THE

Washington Wits

THE

Washington Wits

EDITED BY

BILL ADLER

The Macmillan Company, NEW YORK

Library of Congress Catalog Card Number: 67-13584

FIRST PRINTING

THE MACMILLAN COMPANY, NEW YORK
COLLIER-MACMILLAN CANADA LTD., TORONTO, ONTARIO

PRINTED IN THE UNITED STATES OF AMERICA

I wish to express my appreciation
to my fine staff—
David Curtis, Elaine Crane, and Catherine Johnston—
for their assistance in the preparation of this book,
and to thank James Stroman
for his contributions
to the material herein.

Contents

Introduction

WASHINGTON, D.C., is the capital—literally the head—of the United States, and, like so many responsible heads in this tense and trying era, it is often in need of diversion. Unlike the capital cities of most large nations, Washington was founded, was built, and exists today almost solely for the business of carrying on the affairs of the republic. Perhaps this fact can help to explain the enormous and continuous pressures focused upon the public officials working there. Crises seem daily occurrences, and imminent catastrophe has become a way of life. Obviously, a city like Washington must have a safety valve; otherwise, it could develop a "headache" that would be felt around the world.

Fortunately, such a condition is not a present danger. Washington people have always been blessed with the ability to laugh—at themselves if possible, at others when possible. Taking oneself too seriously is usually a mistake. For a politician, it can often be most "unpolitic." And, for an entire governmental body, it could prove paralyzing. Nothing can put an issue in its proper perspective, or clear the highly charged air, like a good dose of humor.

Thus, throughout our history, guffaws have shattered the still sanctity of the President's office, snickers have invaded the most solemn of high-level conferences, and waves of mirth have drowned out the most momentous of Congressional debates. No one escapes the leveling glance of wit, which might justly be called the most democratic part of the entire government.

The Washington Wits collects for your enjoyment the best of that rich treasury of humor stored up by the current company of public leaders. The selections were culled from speeches, press conferences, interviews, and off-the-cuff remarks made everywhere from the White House rose garden to the Amazon jungles. Represented are the comic quips, the splendid squelches, the well-aimed shafts, and even the occasional outbursts of nonsense that all characterize Washington humor. Political wit can be an effective tool, and an even more potent weapon. But, hopefully, we have presented here a sampling of humor that cuts across all party lines and plays such an indispensable role in helping our nation's capital keep its political balance.

BILL ADLER
New York City

THE

Washington Wits

I. Robert F. Kennedy and the Kennedy Wit

❡ WE MIGHT BE justified in supposing that humor, like many other personality traits, is an identifiable family characteristic. At least this supposition would appear to hold true for the Kennedy family. John F. Kennedy captured the nation's fancy with his warm, vigorous sense of humor and his keenly perceptive wit. Now, with Robert stepping each day more and more before the public eye, the nation is awakening to the bright and probing wit of another Kennedy.

To say that both men possess ready wits, however, is by no means to equate the two, for their senses of humor differ as much as the personalities of the men themselves. We see in Robert Kennedy's humor much of his brother's superior mental agility, that ability to stand a situation on its ear with a deftly timed quip. We find much of the same capacity to withdraw momentarily from involvement in events, in order to obtain that vital objectivity that produces both wit and wisdom. Yet, on the other hand, Robert Kennedy's humor seems to contain a greater flavor of sarcasm, laced perhaps with a touch of the sardonic, and is characterized by a tough, dynamic spirit.

Comparisons of the Kennedy brothers are inevitable, but we must not fail to distinguish their differences. It is hoped that this broad sampling of wit may enable us to grasp another facet of the personality of Robert Kennedy as an individual.

⟨ Senator Robert F. Kennedy, noting that a close relationship exists between politics and the stage in New York State, suggested in 1965 that several prominent figures in the political life of the state might readily fit into Broadway.

"For instance," said Bobby, "John Lindsay starring in *All in Good Time*; Adam Clayton Powell as the lead in *Catch Me if You Can*; Mayor Wagner and Governor Rockefeller in *The Odd Couple* or *Two for the Seesaw*; Senator Javits in *Fade Out-Fade In*; and Winthrop Aldrich is being groomed for the lead in *The Man from UNCLE*.

"Finally," added the Senator, "they're writing a new version of *Luv*, costarring President Johnson and me."

⟨ In Watertown, New York, during his 1964 campaign for the Senate, Robert F. Kennedy took special note of one sign held by a rather unfriendly-looking little boy: "Don't use *me* in your cynical power grab," read the sign.

⟨[Addressing the Baseball Writers' dinner early in 1965, Bobby Kennedy got right into the swing of things:

"I can't believe all those things Ted Williams says about you fellows are true.

"Since my election, I've received many invitations for speaking engagements—from the Overseas Press Club to the Puerto Rican forum. It seems they want me to speak everywhere but on the floor of the Senate.

"I am delighted to see Johnny Keane here tonight—he's new to New York—I'm his guide.

"One of the writers here said that last November I stole home and it wasn't even my home. Being originally from Massachusetts, I was automatically a Yankee. But during the last campaign, I kept hearing 'Yankee, go home.'

"I'm also glad to see Yogi Berra here. I understand he is writing a book: *Lucky To Be a Yankee.* By Yogi Berra, as told to Mel Allen.

"I've also been talking to Joe Cronin. I remember in 1961, when Dave Powers, who is a great baseball fan, brought Joe Cronin into President Kennedy's office to present the traditional baseball pass. President Kennedy said, 'Dave, what was that story you told me about Joe Cronin?'

"Dave looked at Cronin and said, 'Lifetime average of .302?'

"The President said, 'No.'

" 'Hall of Fame?'

"The President said, 'No.'

" 'Mr. President, you must mean the time Carl Hubbell struck out five Hall of Famers in a row—Ruth, Gehrig, Foxx, Simmons, and Joe Cronin.'

" 'Yes, that's the story.'

"And Joe said, 'Mr. President, it's a pleasure to strike out in such company.'

"I enjoy baseball, and I found last year's pennant races

very exciting. In the National League, they couldn't decide who the leader was until the very last day. It sounds like the New York Legislature.

"A number of people here have asked me about that situation. I want to make it clear that there is no truth to reports that I am manager of the Albany Democrats.

"What they're doing up there reminds me of the time when Wilbert Robinson was managing the Brooklyn Dodgers, and three of them arrived at third base at the same time. They asked Uncle Robbie whether he was upset. He said, 'Hell, no, that's the closest those fellows have been to each other all season.'

"I have nine children now—enough for a baseball team. We'll be training soon. Maybe Frank Lane will buy us.

"With all these children I've decided to run my house like the Senate. We have a new speaker. We're working on a Medicare program. But the rest of the family doesn't seem to want to follow the seniority rule.

"The other day a bell rang and I got ready to go to vote. But Ethel said it was just the signal for the four o'clock feeding. . . .

"Speaking seriously, baseball has been our national sport for almost a hundred years. Other sports may be faster, or more exciting on television, but baseball is much more than a spectator sport. When you go out on a nice day, in every playground and vacant lot you will find them playing baseball. It is a part of every man's life. It is a part of our country and will continue to be. As Grantland Rice once said, 'From one old cat to the last at bat.'

"Some say that baseball is on the way down. But as long as young boys have heroes, and as long as the players and owners and all of you meet your responsibilities, I think baseball is on the way up.

"Finally, let me say that I did not run for the Senate to

become Commissioner of Baseball. I'm not interested in the position because it doesn't have enough power."

⟪ The newly elected New York Democratic Senator Robert F. Kennedy was at the very end of the line for Senate seats. Quipped the Senator, "I had better seats for *Hello, Dolly!*"

⟪ Speaking to the Women's National Press Club dinner in January, 1965, Robert Kennedy playfully twitted his reputation as a "carpetbagger" in New York State. "I can't tell you how happy I am to be here representing the great state of . . . ah . . . ah . . ."

⟪ Robert Kennedy's 1964 Senatorial campaign planners told him that their intention was to present him to the television viewers as a sincere, generous person.
   "You going to use a double?" asked Kennedy.

⟪ During the 1964 Presidential campaign, Robert Kennedy made a few remarks to resort patrons at Grossinger's in New York State. "The Catskills were immortalized by Washington Irving. He wrote of a man who fell asleep and awoke in another era. The only other area that can boast such a man is Phoenix, Arizona. . . . Barry Goldwater wants to give control of nuclear weapons to commanders in the field. Now that's my idea of high adventure. General Eisenhower says that he could *live* with a Goldwater Administration. Well, I suppose he'd have as good a chance as anyone else."

⟨ Robert Kennedy asked a reporter if he would be joining him on his 1964 campaign tour of upstate New York. The reporter told him that he would miss the trip because he would be in Boston at the time.

"Never heard of it," deadpanned Kennedy.

⟨ Senator Robert Kennedy, speaking on the subject of foreign aid before the International Radio and TV Society in 1965, urged that assistance in "programs of family planning" be given to foreign nations if requested. At this point Kennedy, father of nine children, interrupted himself, turned to his wife, Ethel, and said, "You'd better leave."

⟨ Addressing the Women's National Press Club dinner for the new Congress in 1965, Robert Kennedy made light of his reputed ambition. "I want to assure you I have no Presidential aspirations—nor does my wife, Ethel Bird."

⟨ Robert Kennedy's daughter Kerry once impetuously embraced her father and kissed him vigorously on the cheek. Admonished Bobby, laughing, "Please Kerry, I told you—only when there are cameramen around."

⟨ Outbursts of political humor know no geographical confines. On a 1965 South American tour, Robert Kennedy was swimming alongside an Indian canoe when he announced resonantly, in imitation of a radio commentator, "It was impossible to pinpoint the time when he decided to run for President, but the idea seemed to take hold as he was swimming in the Amazonian river of Nhamunda, keeping an eye out for the man-eating piranhas."

He thought for a moment, and then added, "Piranhas have never been known to bite a U.S. Senator."

◖ In Rome, recalls Robert F. Kennedy, "We had a friendly audience with Pope John. . . . He blessed us all, including the American newspapermen who were traveling with us, most of whom were not Catholics. He assured them that it was just a little blessing and wouldn't do them any harm."

◖ New York Senatorial candidate Robert Kennedy sent a sample of his cramped and barely legible handwriting to a handwriting analyst late in 1964. The sample read, "If you tell your readers what you see in my handwriting, you'll cost me the election."

◖ After an unhappy incident at a television studio during Robert Kennedy's 1964 Senatorial campaign, a network official was attempting to smooth things over a bit. "We just try to do our best," he explained.

"That's all right," returned Kennedy. "We'll try to make up for your shortcomings."

◖ During his Senatorial campaign in 1964, Robert Kennedy met with an exuberant crowd in Buffalo, New York. Overenthusiastic supporters screamed and pushed, trying to get close enough to touch the candidate or shake his hand. At a milder reception that evening, Kennedy joked, "I've been all over the state talking Medicare today and when I came into Buffalo tonight I thought I needed it myself."

◖ Robert Kennedy got the most enthusiastic reception of his whole 1964 Senatorial campaign in Rochester, New York, where thousands of screaming supporters lined the streets. Standing atop his car, Bobby placidly observed, "There's nothing like a quiet evening in Rochester."

◖ In January, 1965, Edward M. Kennedy gave his brother, Robert, a lift to Capitol Hill, where the newly elected New York Senator was about to make his legislative debut. Cracked Bobby, taking the wheel, "Which way do I drive, Eddie? You know this routine now."

◖ In a 1964 campaign stopover in Johnson City, New York, whose largest industry is the manufacture of shoes, Robert Kennedy noted, "I've done two important things for the shoe industry. First of all, eight small children need a lot of shoes. And second, I'm the one who popularized those fifty-mile hikes."

◖ Reasoned Robert Kennedy during his 1964 campaign for Senator in New York, "I lived in New York for many years, but if this election is to be decided on the basis of who's lived here the longest, perhaps we should just elect the oldest man in the state."

◖ A large crowd welcomed RFK at the Syracuse, New York, airport during the candidate's 1964 campaign. As Kennedy moved down the line, shaking hands, the crowd appeared to grow rather than shrink. Finally he discovered the explanation: "As soon as they shake my hand, they run to the end of the line."

⟨ Again replying to charges of carpetbagging in the 1964 Senatorial election, Robert Kennedy stated, "I was raised in New York and went to school here. If somebody's going to vote against me because of my accent, there's really nothing I can do about it. It's really a Glen Cove accent, you know."

⟨ At 3:30 A.M. on the morning following his election to the Senate in 1964, Robert F. Kennedy fulfilled his promise to come back to his first stop on the campaign trail—the Fulton Fish Market on Manhattan's Lower East Side. Whiffed Kennedy, "It smells a lot better down here now."

⟨ Robert Kennedy's decision to run for the Senatorial seat from New York State weighed heavily upon him. The possibility of defeat worried him, and, as he said in August, 1964, "I don't want to become a retired elder statesman at thirty-eight."

⟨ There were some complaints in 1964 that Attorney General Robert Kennedy had chosen to run for Senator from New York at the request of the state's "bosses." In one city hundreds of people jammed the lobby of the hotel at which Kennedy was staying, and the candidate quipped, "I am delighted to see so many bosses here to welcome me."

⟨ At Batavia, New York, one of Robert Kennedy's 1964 Senatorial campaign stops, a group of six young girls from the nearby town of Kennedy were in attendance. "You see?" said the Democratic candidate. "They talk about my being a carpetbagger and I even have a *city* named after me."

❲ On a campaign stop in Ossining, New York, less than two weeks from the day of the Senatorial election in 1964, Robert Kennedy once more made light of the charges of carpetbagging by his opponent, Senator Kenneth Keating. "Who grew up in Westchester County? I did. Keating didn't. Does Ken Keating know the problems of Westchester County? No. Boo-Boo, Ken Keating! Boo-Boo. Did he go to Bronxville schools as I did? No. Keating is the carpetbagger. He says keep New York's own. Imagine that. Boo-Boo, Ken Keating. Boo-Boo. Do you want a local boy in the U.S. Senate? That's me! There's even some talk about Keating dumping garbage in the Hudson River."

❲ His plane circling the landing field at one city, during his 1964 Senatorial campaign, Robert Kennedy excitedly gazed down at the crowd that had gathered to greet him. "Look down there," he said enthusiastically, "I think I see two people who are over twenty-one."

❲ Robert Kennedy made his 1964 Senatorial campaign debut at New York City's Fulton Fish Market, promising, "I have eight children, and we eat fish every Friday. From now on, we'll eat fish twice a week. That's what we're going to do for the fishing industry of New York."

❲ Thumbing through a promotional pamphlet prepared for his 1964 Senatorial campaign, Attorney General Robert

Kennedy came across a photograph of himself shaking hands with a well-known labor leader.

"There must be a better photo than this," said Kennedy to the advertising men in charge of his campaign.

"What's wrong with this one?" asked one adman.

"That fellow's in jail," said Attorney General.

❨ Robert F. Kennedy's "image," prior to his 1964 Senatorial campaign in New York, was that of a ruthless, callous politician, and the success of the campaign depended on his ability to overcome and to change that image. After the election a reporter asked him if he was relieved that it was all over. Bobby replied in the affirmative, adding, "Now I can go back to being ruthless again."

❨ Several celebrities held an outdoor campaign rally for Robert F. Kennedy one late-summer evening in 1964. It was a high-spirited affair, during which Bobby joined his friend Sammy Davis, Jr., at the microphone for a duet and remarked, "If things don't go well on November third, we can go on tour."

❨ Robert F. Kennedy appeared on Barry Gray's New York radio program during his candidacy for the Senate in 1964. During the interview Gray noted that the show had a large audience, to which Kennedy replied, "I always knew you had a large audience, everywhere I go in this state there's a group of people shouting, 'We want Barry.'"

❨ In one city along the New York State campaign trail during 1964, Robert Kennedy addressed the young people in the crowd. "Back in the last town, I saw a sign that read, 'Respectable Young People for Keating.' Well, I don't know where that leaves you."

⟨ *The New York Times* supported Republican Senator Kenneth Keating in New York's 1964 election, but Robert Kennedy shrugged it off. "Well, at least they can never say I got my job through *The New York Times.*"

⟨ Late in the 1964 Senatorial campaign, Robert Kennedy was a guest at a cocktail party attended by the political columnists of New York's newspapers and magazines. A young woman approached him, announcing, "I'm with the New York *Post* and this is my first campaign."

"Mine too," replied Kennedy. "We'd better stay together."

⟨ Robert Kennedy began one of his 1964 Senatorial campaign speeches with this statement: "A few months ago I was having breakfast with my wife. And I was reading in the papers that California had replaced New York as the number-one state in population—so I turned to my wife and I said, 'What can we *do?*' So I moved to New York, and in just one day I increased the population by ten and a half—my opponent has just sixty days to match that record."

⟨ In Riverdale, Long Island, the issue of carpetbagging in the 1964 Senatorial campaign was raised once again when a young lad shouted at Robert Kennedy, "Go back where you came from." Replied Kennedy, "People have been telling me that all week—and that's why I'm here."

❨ Robert Kennedy counted the Goldwater signs in the crowd at a 1964 campaign rally in Riverdale, New York: "One, two, three, four, five, six—I've been all up and down the state and that's the most Goldwater people I've seen in one place. I think they were flown in from Albany."

❨ Robert Kennedy's reception in Jamestown, New York, during the 1964 Senatorial campaign was quite enthusiastic. Cracked Bobby, "I see my Long Island accent got you."

As the candidate was addressing the crowd at the airport, the takeoff of a commercial airliner drowned out his speech. Indicating the offending jet, Kennedy added, "He's on his way back to Phoenix to report."

❨ On a 1964 campaign stop in the birthplace of Senator Kenneth Keating, Robert Kennedy paused to needle his Republican opponent. "It gives me a deep sense of satisfaction to come here to Rochester, since I know it is the home town of a distinguished white-haired American . . . and I am referring, of course, to Susan B. Anthony."

❨ Economical citizens of Massena, New York, converted their "Welcome Ted Kennedy" signs to "Welcome Bob Kennedy" by stapling the new pasteboard name over the old. Noticing this situation, Bob tore his name off one sign and, holding it up to the crowd, stated, "There's one big advantage to electing me. It will be cheaper for everybody. We can interchange signs with Massachusetts."

❲ Arriving several hours behind schedule for a 1964 campaign rally in Glens Falls, New York, Robert Kennedy found the crowd still waiting for him. Thanking them for their patience, Kennedy sighed: "Well, here we are five hours late. That's the well-oiled Kennedy machine for you."

❲ Robert Kennedy was informed by the advertising agency handling his 1964 campaign for New York Senator that although there were only three "fliers" in actual distribution, another thirty-eight layouts were in preparation for distribution. Noted Kennedy, "Another week and you won't have to print anything. You can hand out the layouts."

❲ Following his election as Senator in 1964, Robert Kennedy was invited to meet the editorial staff of a New York City newspaper that had endorsed his Republican opponent, Kenneth Keating, and had criticized him through the campaign. Addressing the solemn assemblage, Kennedy began, "First of all, I want to thank each and every one of you for your support."

❲ In July, 1964, Robert F. Kennedy was asked about the possibility of his entering Massachusetts politics. Shaking his head, Kennedy replied, "I'd be a carpetbagger there."

⟪ Prior to his moving to Riverdale, New York, in 1964, Robert Kennedy had resided in Brookline, Massachusetts, but during the Senatorial campaign he had to explain, "Averell [Harriman] got that a little mixed up the other night. He introduced me at a Brooklyn rally as a local boy."

⟪ Along with his mother, wife, and sisters, Robert F. Kennedy frequently contributed to the various political campaigns of his brother John. During one of them he treated the crowd at a rally to one of the most direct political pronouncements on record: "My brother Jack couldn't be here. My mother couldn't be here. My sister Eunice couldn't be here, my sister Pat couldn't be here, my sister Jean couldn't be here, but if my brother Jack were here he'd tell you Lodge has a very bad voting record."

⟪ Bobby Kennedy, who plays his family's touch football games to win, discounts all accusations that he changes the rules in mid-game: "They only complain about the rules because they always lose."

⟪ In Saranac, New York, a woman mistakenly boarded the Kennedy family plane and was quite flustered to find seated there Mrs. John F. Kennedy, Robert Kennedy, and a number of children. Remarked Robert later, "She was a very nice woman, but she thought it was very crowded for a commercial plane."

⟪ After formally declaring his candidacy for the 1964 Senate nomination in New York, Robert F. Kennedy was asked if this were the first time that he had ever run for public office. Answered Kennedy, ingenuously, "Yes, but I've had a couple of relatives who did."

⟨ On the day that John F. Kennedy was elected President in 1960, the family played touch football at their Hyannis Port home. Bobby played quarterback, and brother Jack went downfield for a pass. Jack was gathering in the pass but, with the unawed defense closing in on him, dropped it. Noted Robert, "That's my brother. All guts, no brains."

⟨ Democratic candidate Robert Kennedy won the New York Senatorial election in 1964 by taking 55 per cent of the vote. Calling his brother, Ted, in Massachusetts on election night, he gibed, "A little bit of what I did down here is rubbing off on you. What per cent of the vote are you getting up there? 81 per cent?"

⟨ In a moment of unexcelled candor and humility, Robert F. Kennedy confessed in early 1963, "To be quite frank, there is tremendous advantage in having the same last name as the President of the United States—but—I think a lot can be accomplished even when you are not related to the President."

⟨ Asked in January, 1963, if being the President's brother was not difficult for him at times, Robert Kennedy replied, "I don't find it so. It might be for him, but it isn't for me."

❨ Noted Robert Kennedy in January, 1963, "I've been associated with the present incumbent in the White House for thirty-seven years, the first few of which were slow."

❨ Robert Kennedy had serious doubts about the post of Attorney General, but once he had convinced himself, he was invulnerable to criticism from others. In a phone conversation with President Kennedy early in 1961, Bobby jokingly paraphrased a noted Eisenhower defense of Sherman Adams: "Why don't you say I may be your brother, but you need me?"

❨ Visitors to Attorney General Robert Kennedy's office were shown a picture of RFK's son David on the White House lawn, with President Kennedy's autographed inscription reading, "A future President inspects his property." Noted Bobby, "That proves there's a dynasty."

❨ The 1960 West Virginia Presidential primary ended in a landslide victory for John Kennedy. Soon after the polls had closed, Ethel Kennedy began snapping pictures and asking everyone, delightedly, "Isn't it exciting?" Cracked Robert Kennedy to reporters, "I couldn't have done it without my brother."

❨ Robert F. Kennedy solemnly addressed the graduating class at Marquette University: "Years ago, I was a hardworking lawyer making $4,200 a year. I took my work home every night and was very diligent. Ten years later I became the Attorney General of the United States. So, you see, if you want to become successful, just get your brother elected President."

([Not especially famed for his rhetorical prowess, Robert Kennedy once ran into difficulty in addressing the Foreign Student Service Council. Attempting to turn one of John's most famous phrases, Bob began, "You people are exemplifying what my brother meant when he said in his inaugural address, 'Ask what you can do for—uh—uh—do not ask what you can do—uh—ask not what you can do for your country but——' Well, anyhow, you remember his words."

The listeners laughed loudly, and Bob added, "That's why my brother is President."

([During a 1964 press conference Robert Kennedy was asked if he would accept the Vice-Presidential nomination, and he answered, "The question reminds me of my brother. When he was posed with such a question, he used to say that is like asking a girl if she would marry that man if he proposed."

([A Justice Department lawyer who was referring to a business run downhill by a son drew this observation from Robert Kennedy in 1963: "That's one mistake our father never made—taking us into business with him."

([Erroneously receiving a phone call for a "Senator Kennedy" in early 1963, Robert F. sighed. "That's how it goes. First they mistook me for Jack, and now, Teddy."

❪ During the 1964 Senatorial campaign both Robert ˈand Ethel Kennedy were once surrounded by autograph hounds. Bob succeeded in disengaging himself first and, reaching the car, watched for a minute as his wife continued to sign autographs. "Ethel," he finally reminded her, "I'm the candidate."

❪ In refutation of the charges that he was the 1964 Senatorial candidate of the bosses, Robert F. Kennedy stated, "I have only one boss and she's at home."

❪ Prior to 1960, Mrs. Arthur Schlesinger, Jr., was a supporter of Adlai Stevenson. Demanded Robert Kennedy of the vexed Mr. Schlesinger, "Can't you control your own wife, or are you like me?"

❪ In 1961, wondering about the right present for his young son David's sixth birthday, Robert Kennedy mused, "He wants a billy goat, and my wife got him one, unfortunately. My second son, Bobby, collects animals. He's also a junior botanist. Bobby picks up bees with his fingers. I caught two turtles for him while riding last Sunday, to fill out the collection we've got at home—chicks, geese, horses, ponies, tadpoles, frogs, lizards, birds, cats, puppies, and dogs. I got a seal for the children for Christmas two years ago. He escaped once and was found by the milkman in the middle of town and had to be captured by the local police. This seal got to be real friendly, but when he found out food came from the kitchen he was always trying to get into the kitchen, so we had to give him to the zoo. We had a deodorized skunk once, but it escaped while being transported from Hyannis Port to Washington and is still missing. A friend brought Bobby a toad the other day for his collection, half of which is kept in the house, the other half out."

The collection, or the toad?

❲ A trip for the Robert Kennedys is generally an operation of considerable magnitude. Lining up the children one day, Bobby informed them, "We're all going to a convention— now be good. I have something for the one who's best."

As the youngsters turned to march off, Kennedy added, "And one more thing—I'll *also* have something for the one who's worst."

❲ During Senator Robert Kennedy's tour of South America late in 1965, the Kennedy plane was en route from Brazil to Caracas, Venezuela, when this announcement was made by the pilot over the intercom: "Senator and Mrs. Kennedy, it has been a great pleasure to have you aboard. We are now crossing the Brazilian-Venezuelan border, and it is time to say good-bye."

Startled, the Senator turned to his wife and asked, "What's he going to do, get off here?"

Safely on the ground, Kennedy addressed the Caracas crowds from the roof of his embassy car:

"I want you all to know how nice it is for me and my wife to be in Caracas." (Applause.) "We in the United States have a great admiration and a great affection for the people of Venezuela." (Applause.)

He then added, "I want to say to my young friends— Venezuela will continue to make progress if you're ready to stay in school. And you'll be spanked by your mother if you don't." (Laughter.)

⟦ Robert F. Kennedy told this story on his 1962 visit to Tokyo: "A man asked for a judgeship for his brother. I declined—I received the inevitable phone call. He said, 'After all, your brother appointed you Attorney General.'

"I answered, 'We only serve the will of the President.' "

⟦ As Robert Kennedy finished his speech at Waseda University during his 1962 visit to Japan, a young cheerleader stepped forward to lead the students in their school song. Kennedy reports that "During the first chorus he accidently struck my wife in the pit of the stomach. She said it didn't hurt, or at least not nearly so much as it would have if he hadn't been a friend."

⟦ Robert Kennedy was accorded a tumultuous welcome in Poland, and in Cracow the mayor asked if he intended to run for President of the United States. Quipped Kennedy, "No, I don't think I'll run for President. I think I'll run for mayor of Cracow."

⟦ On a trip to Korea, Robert Kennedy was briefed by an Army general. Bob later remarked to a friend, "I don't want to worry you. But you remember that general who explained how we would handle the North Koreans if they attacked? Well, the last time I saw him was two years ago in Berlin when he told us what we would do if the Russians ever moved in on us there. The only other time I saw him was when he was holding a briefing on the Bay of Pigs operation."

◖ Robert Kennedy and his wife attended Sunday mass at St. John's Cathedral during their stay in Warsaw, Poland. Some 5,000 enthusiastic Poles surrounded his car after the services, and Bobby observed, "This is the way we always come home from mass."

◖ During his 1962 visit to Japan, at a Buddhist temple in Osaka, a priest gave Robert Kennedy a stick of incense to burn. Kennedy asked Ambassador Edwin O. Reischauer if such a gesture were permissible, and Reischauer indicated that it was merely a demonstration of respect.

"You're sure it won't look as if I'm worshiping Buddha?" asked the Roman Catholic Kennedy. Reischauer again assured him that it was all right. Kennedy picked up the incense, still muttering, "If I get kicked out——"

◖ During an official visit to Japan in 1962, Robert Kennedy confided in a group of foreign correspondents in Tokyo, "I had seaweed for breakfast yesterday. To tell you the honest-to-goodness truth it didn't taste bad. When I went to Central Asia with Justice Douglas in 1955, they brought in a goat, very dead, plucked out its eyes, and served them to us. Justice Douglas turned to me and said, 'For the sake of America, Bob, make like it's an oyster!' So things have gone up since then."

◖ The Democratic Senator from New York recounts this incident at Japan's Nihon University, where in 1962 "there were no heating facilities in the building but the university officials made arrangements to keep at least one part of us warn by placing electric cushions on our chairs. This can be slightly disconcerting, especially if it feels too warm and you can't find the switch to turn it off."

⟨ The enormous crowds that greeted Robert Kennedy in Poland once caused him to be late for a dinner. Polish Communist officials, infuriated by Kennedy's "playing to the crowds," reproved him, saying, "Premier Gomulka never does."

Replied Kennedy, "Well, maybe that's the problem."

⟨ Robert Kennedy's Japanese visit in 1962 did hold one uncomfortable recollection for him. "It did seem embarrassing to me to come to the end of a meeting with the Foreign Minister of Japan and then suddenly thrust on him an autographed photograph of myself. I could imagine his sick smile as he opened it and said, 'Just what I always wanted . . .' (When I gave the picture to one of the ministers, I told him that at least it was a nice frame and that he could take my picture out and replace it with one of his wife. He laughed, slightly nervously, I thought, as if I had read his own thoughts.)"

⟨ During Robert F. Kennedy's speech at the University of Mississippi early in 1966, a question was raised concerning the incidents involving the Negro James Meredith's admission to the school several years before. The New York Senator divulged some of the behind-the-scenes maneuvering that took place preceding the disorders. He revealed that as Attorney General he had held about twenty-five telephone conversations with Mississippi Governor Ross Barnett, who had asked him to send federal marshals with orders to draw their guns. It would thus appear to Mississipians that Barnett was relenting only in the face of the Federal Government's superior force.

Related Kennedy, "I said I would have the Chief Marshal pull his gun. He called back in a little while and said

he had talked with his advisers in Jackson, and *all* the marshals would have to pull their guns."

⟮ As one of the speakers at a 1966 luncheon for the Fed-
eration of Jewish Philanthropies, Senator Robert F. Kennedy was faced with the necessity of following the eloquent
barrister Louis Nizer to the rostrum. Describing his feelings
on the occasion Bobby told this story by way of analogy: "A
man bored everyone he met by relating his experiences
during the Johnstown flood. . . . When he died, he asked
Saint Peter to gather an audience so that he could tell them
his story of the Johnstown flood. Saint Peter agreed, but
warned him: 'Remember, Noah will be in the audience.' "

⟮ When, in 1963, Robert Kennedy was asked if he would
care to guess who would be nominated as the Republican
candidate for President in 1964, he replied, "Well, I know,
but I don't think he does, so I don't think I'd better say."

⟮ As he was leaving the Overseas Press Club one night,
Robert Kennedy was suddenly surrounded by a group of
nuns. Disengaging himself, he remarked, "It's one of the
great unsolved mysteries. All the nuns love me and none of
the priests do."

⟮ Robert F. Kennedy's diligence often keeps him at work
even on holidays. One year, on Washington's Birthday,
Bob was gratified to see a number of automobiles parked in
the Justices' parking places, and he noted their license
numbers in order to write each of them a letter of appreciation. One reply confessed, "I cannot tell a lie on Washing-

ton's Birthday—I used my parking space but I went to the movies."

"With honesty like yours," Kennedy responded, "our country's cherry trees are safe."

❲ In 1964 Robert Kennedy had decided to take a week off for a skiing trip, but he became a little suspicious when a visitor told him that he was glad he was getting away. Queried Kennedy, "You're the ninth person to tell me that today. What's everybody plotting here, a palace coup?"

❲ Robert Kennedy enjoys teasing his Republican co-Senator Jacob Javits whenever the opportunity arises. Learning that they were both scheduled to appear at a rally protesting Soviet anti-Semitism, Kennedy asked Javits if he would care to write a fitting speech for him. Javits readily agreed, but Bobby needled him a little more. "Will you embrace me up there, just as though I were John Lindsay?"

❲ The Robert Kennedys had planned to hold a gala reception for delegates following the 1964 Nominating Convention. All the arrangements were studiously completed— except for the mailing of the delegates' invitations. When the error was discovered, the "Kennedy hostesses" began to invite passersby in off the street. Finally learning of the blunder, Kennedy only winced and said, "I knew there was something wrong. Not enough people were wearing delegate badges, and too many were carrying boxes marked Macy's."

❲ RFK recalls the glorious moments in 1965 before he began his ascent of the final ridge on the way to the peak of Mt. Kennedy—the steepest part of the climb: "I remembered my mother's last words to me: 'Don't slip, dear,' and the admonition of a friend who had obviously never climbed: 'Don't look down.' And I remembered what my son, Joe, said on the telephone as I was about to leave Seattle: 'Good luck, Daddy. You'll need it.' And the reporter from a national newspaper covering the climb told me before I began that his paper had just completed my obituary. All of these splendid thoughts raced through my mind."

❲ Robert Kennedy's candid remarks upon his climbing of Mt. Kennedy in 1965 are heroic only in their hilarity. "I am no mountain climber. My family has always shared an active interest in all sorts of athletic endeavor, but I personally never had thought of climbing a mountain. Frankly, I don't like heights."

❲ Teamster boss Jimmy Hoffa, who had more than a passing acquaintance with Robert Kennedy, attempted to rally his powerful union against the Kennedy family and was joined by several other union leaders. When the notorious Brooklyn gangster Joey Gallo asked RFK if his influence might be of some help in the campaign, Bobby replied, "Just tell everybody you're voting for Nixon."

❲ When New York's Republican Governor Rockefeller opposed a bill that would raise the state minimum wage to $1.50 per hour, Bobby Kennedy took the opportunity to rib the state leader. RFK pointed out that he had nine

children, and added ironically, "I know *I* couldn't get by on
$1.50 an hour and I doubt if Mr. Rockefeller could."

❲ Attorney General Robert Kennedy's office was responsible for "requesting" contributions from American businessmen for the liberation of Castro's prisoners from Cuba in
1962. According to Kennedy, some businessmen made
donations because they were humanitarians, some because
they would be able to compensate through tax adjustments,
and some, noted the Attorney General wryly, "perhaps felt
they'd like to have a warmer relationship with the Government."

❲ As Attorney General, in 1962 Robert Kennedy was
once asked of the whereabouts of an old "acquaintance,"
Dave Beck. "He's on parole," answered Kennedy. "He's
working at the parking lot he owns in Seattle. He's the one
who comes up to the car and says, 'One hour—that'll be
seventy-five cents, please.' "

❲ During the violent civil rights disorders at Oxford, Mississippi, in 1962, an aide telephoning then-Attorney General Robert Kennedy reported that the harried Justice
Department officers on the university campus felt like the
defenders of the Alamo. "Well," remarked Kennedy, "you
know what happened to those guys."

❲ Robert F. Kennedy was strictly *non grata* in Portland,
Oregon, after he initiated a rather unpopular investigation
there in 1957. The feeling was not wholly unreciprocated,
and as Kennedy's plane landed there in 1962, the Attorney

General turned to his companions and said, "Let's jump out, punch the first guy we see in the nose, jump right back into this thing, and get out of here."

(A teen-ager asked Robert Kennedy why he left Riverdale, New York, as a young child. Explained RFK, "I didn't want to leave. I was three years old at the time and I pleaded with my mother, 'Why must we leave Riverdale?' But we left anyway."

(As Senator Robert Kennedy was finishing a speech honoring forty-three graduates of a VISTA training program in August, 1965, one of the trainees suggested that he officially swear them in. Learning that there was no official oath of office, Kennedy smiled and improvised: "Repeat after me. I swear that I will be a good VISTA volunteer. I will assist those in need, help my U.S. Senator all I can, and otherwise behave myself. So help me God."

(Senator Robert Kennedy and union leader Jimmy Hoffa have never been on the most cordial of terms. When asked what he thought of Hoffa's talk of organizing major league baseball players, Kennedy responded, "I hope he doesn't get to first base."

(Attorney General Robert Kennedy arrived late at a Business Council Meeting in the Capitol, and with a straight face he attributed the delay to "a suit filed by the Dupont Company to require the Justice Department to divest itself of the Antitrust Division."

❲ At a Washington party celebrating his twenty-fifth year as head of the federal prison system, James Bennett was slicing his cake when he struck something hard. Probing around in the cake, Bennett finally extracted the object: an eight-inch file, placed there by . . . Robert F. Kennedy.

❲ En route to Assumption College in Worcester, Massachusetts, where he was to accept an honorary degree, Robert Kennedy encountered some firm pressure from his wife to get a haircut. Finally, on the way from the airport to the college, Ethel decided that the tonsorial appointment could no longer be postponed.

As the Kennedys, police escort and all, trooped into the barber shop, a woman passerby observed, "I have to chloroform my seven-year-old to get his hair cut. This guy has to have a cop."

❲ Attorney General Robert Kennedy and Postmaster General J. Edward Day were speaking on the same platform on one occasion, and Day mentioned that half of the country's 35,000 postmasters were women. When Kennedy rose to speak, he began, "It's all right about 50 per cent of postmasters being women, but I think it is even more important that only 5 per cent of the inmates of our federal prisons are women."

❲ When, in August, 1964, President Lyndon Johnson ruled out all Cabinet members as possible candidates for Vice-Presidential nomination, many observers interpreted the move as a way of specifically eliminating Robert F. Kennedy (then Attorney General) without offending his partisans.

Soon thereafter Kennedy, addressing a school for Congressional candidates, commented, "I must confess I stand in awe of you. You are not members of the Cabinet. Therefore you are eligible for Vice-President. I've decided to send a little note to Cabinet members in general, saying, 'I'm sorry I took so many nice fellows over the side with me.'"

(Attorney General Robert Kennedy was attending a party for Abraham Ribicoff, who had resigned his post as Secretary of Health, Education, and Welfare to run for the Senate in Connecticut. Ribicoff mentioned that it had been hard for him to retain the image of a moderate Democrat during his campaign because his constituents always associated him with liberals in the Administration such as Orville Freeman, Arthur Goldberg, and Walter Heller. Here Kennedy interjected, "Tell your people back home the President never has any Cabinet meetings and you've never even met any of those fellows."

2. Hubert, the Irrepressible: Vice-President Hubert H. Humphrey

⟨ HUBERT HUMPHREY is widely known for his political acumen, his ingratiating smile, and his almost irresistible "gift of gab." All stand him in good stead in the department of political humor. As we read through Humphrey's collected quips, we can visualize him flashing that boyish grin and taking most of the sting out of his more pointed barbs. He is always prepared for an impromptu speech and always ready with an appropriate off-the-cuff comment. Much of his humor is characterized by a note of irony, especially when referring to himself. And, in his informal speeches, Hubert Humphrey often reveals a satirical flair that identifies him as a political wit of considerable stature.

❨ Vice-President Hubert Humphrey delivered this mono-
logue before an annual Gridiron Club dinner: ". . . and
speaking of humor, it's nice to see Mr. Richard Nixon here
this evening. That is, it's nice to see Mr. Nixon here this
evening . . . as a successful lawyer!

"One thing we must say for Mr. Nixon, he never stops
trying . . . in the past few months he has received more
publicity than anyone in his party. And I would like to
predict that if he keeps it up, Richard Nixon may someday
reach his political goal . . . but don't go by me, because I
once predicted that Senator Everett Dirksen would be an
opera singer!

"Governor Wallace was supposed to be here, but I understand he couldn't make it. It seems he's busy conferring
with Alabama's leading mathematicians, geologists, and
physicists. They're preparing a new simple literacy test for
the voters in Selma!

"But it's a pleasure to see Sargent Shriver here this evening. Mr. Shriver, as you know, holds down two full-time
jobs, and only last week the President was thinking of offering him another one, but I talked him out of it. After all,
we'll never win the war on poverty if one man gets all the
work!

"Personally, I thrive on activity. I enjoy it. I welcome
extra duties. President Johnson knows this, and he's letting
me participate in many programs. I understand this year,
before the President tosses out the first pitch to start the
American League season, he's going to let me rub up the
ball!

"My wife, Muriel, kids me about my activity. The other
night she said to me, 'Daddy, you spend a couple of hours
at home each evening, why waste them? Why don't you
apply for a part-time job at the neighborhood drugstore?'

"I just love to keep myself active and busy. As presiding
officer of the Senate I get to vote in case of a tie. Of course,

there's not too much activity in *that* activity! As a matter of
fact, it can become quite frustrating sitting up there in the
Senate day after day, with your fingers crossed, hoping for
a tie!

"But I can honestly say I'm enjoying my position in the
Senate this year . . . where else would I be able to get an
occasional glimpse of Senator George Murphy without
makeup?

"They tell me that when George Murphy entered the
Senate chambers for the first time, he walked up to a page
and said, 'Where's my dressing room?'

"In a way it's nice to have George Murphy in the Senate.
During a lull in the proceedings he lets me read his *Variety*.

"It's too bad they voted down Mr. Murphy's first proposal. He suggested the Senate innaugurate *late, late sessions!*

"But I understand Senator George Murphy promises to
bring a really new innovation to the Senate. In the future,
when he introduces a Republican measure, he is not going
to get up and talk about it. He's going to present the entire
bill on tape, complete with a laugh track!

"In conclusion, I would like to say this: I will go any
place I am asked to go . . . I will do anything I am asked to
do . . . at any time. Because, after all, they say in that well-
known ad, you have to keep trying harder and harder when
you're only number two!"

⟨ During the taut moments at the 1964 Democratic
Convention when everyone awaited Lyndon Johnson's announcement of a running mate, a local television interviewer waved his microphone avidly in front of Hubert
Humphrey and asked quickly, "Senator, do you know anything? Are you nervous? How are you bearing up?"

Answered Humphrey calmly, "Obviously, a lot better
than you are."

❮[Hubert Humphrey was the first to describe Republicans Everett Dirksen and Charles Halleck's report on the Congress as "The Twilight Zone."

❮[Introducing Humphrey at an NAACP convention, a speaker lauded him as the "John the Baptist of Civil Rights, a voice in the wilderness before the rest of the country woke up." Remarked Humphrey after the introduction, "Well, I guess you all know what happened to John the Baptist."

❮[Humphrey derides government officials who make use of the dependable cliché "in the long run."

"Hell," he exclaims, "in the long run we'll all be dead."

❮[During the Cuban missile crisis of 1962, President Kennedy confided to Hubert Humphrey, "If I'd known the job was this tough, I wouldn't have trounced you in West Virginia."

Said Humphrey to the President, "If I hadn't known it was this tough, I never would have let you beat me."

❮[Vice-President Hubert Humphrey recently addressed the 1966 meeting of the Gridiron Club and displayed a routine not unworthy of a stand-up comedian:

"I am honored to be invited here tonight, not only because it gives me an opportunity to join in the hilarity of the evening, but also because I finally got a chance to wear my Inaugural suit.

"I want to express my profound thanks to those who cleared and approved my speech here tonight—Bill Moyers, Jack Valenti, George Reedy, Lynda Bird, Luci Baines, Luci's third- and fourth-ranking escorts—William S. White.

"As you all may recall, I never sought the job of Vice-President, and I was the most surprised man in Atlantic City when I got the call from the White House.

"You all may remember I rushed out to the airport, and there sitting in the plane was Senator Tom Dodd. And *then*, I was *really* the most surprised man in Atlantic City.

"Anyway, we flew to Washington, and I am now in a position to tell you what went on in the President's office.

"The President looked at me and said, 'Hubert, do you think you can keep your mouth shut for the next four years?' I said, 'Yes, Mr. President,' and he said, 'There you go interrupting me again.'

"Then came the campaign. As most of you remember, it was a very clean campaign, without the usual name-calling that goes with the Presidential election. To this day I have a great deal of respect for Barry Goldwater and his running mate, what's-his-name.

"I only met Barry once during the campaign. It was in Sioux Falls, and we happened to run into each other at the airport. I told him at the time he'd better lay off the Social Security issue, and he replied, 'Listen, you run your campaign and I'll *ruin* mine.'

"On November 5, I got a call from him, and he said, 'And what was that you advised me to do at the airport that day?'

"But I am glad to say that Barry and I are still very good friends and to show that there are no hard feelings, he has promised me a private screening of the film made by the Mothers for Moral America.

"After being elected, I immediately sought out the advice of another great Vice-President, Richard Nixon. I

said, 'Dick, what do I need to be a good Vice-President?'
And he replied, 'Get yourself a good dog.'

" 'And then,' he said, 'you need a crisis.'

"I asked him how many crises did he think I needed, and
he replied, 'At least six.'

" 'What else,' I asked him. And he said, 'Stay the hell out
of South America.'

"There's been a lot written about a residence for the
Vice-President. The truth is that the President asked me
about that. I said, 'Mr. President, I kind of go for those big,
old houses with the columns on them.'

"He said, 'Yes-s-s-s-s . . .'

"I said, 'Mr. President, I like a house that is close in. I
like a lot of yard, a lot of trees and squirrels, and a lot of
driveway. I like a lot of bedrooms in different colors.'

"The President said, 'Yes. . . .'

"And I finally said, 'Mr. President, I think I have my eye
on just the place.'

" 'Well, I can't give you the house, but I tell you what I
will do—I'll send Lady Bird out to your place to plant a
rose bush.'

"But I am glad we didn't get the house anyway because
every time I suggest new quarters, Muriel and my daughter
sit on the floor clasping hands and start singing 'We Shall
Not Be Moved.'

"I have had some interesting assignments since I was
made Vice-President. For one thing, I am chairman of the
War on Poverty. I was first suggested for the job after my
campaign in West Virginia. I remember the President, who
was then Senate majority leader, saying to me after the
primary, 'Youbert, that was the poorest campaign I have
ever seen. If I ever have a poverty program, I am going to
make you head of it.'

"A great deal has been said and written about the role of
the Vice-President of our country and I am frequently

asked if I am disappointed. I want to say here and now for the *record*, I am not in the least disappointed.

"I will admit there are a few things that rankle me. For instance, Mike Mansfield, Russell Long, and Carl Hayden all have sumptuous offices at the Capital. BUT NOT HUBERT HUMPHREY.

"Chief Justice Warren, Dean Rusk, and Dwight Eisenhower were sent to London for the Churchill funeral. BUT NOT HUBERT HUMPHREY.

"Everett Dirksen, Gerry Ford, Bob McNamara, and Sargent Shriver can all talk to the President. BUT NOT HUBERT HUMPHREY.

"Wayne Morse, Bobby Kennedy, and George Murphy can talk in the Senate as long as they please. BUT NOT HUBERT HUMPHREY.

"President Johnson, Stewart Udall, and Pierre Salinger all know how to ride a horse. BUT NOT HUBERT HUMPHREY.

"Now one of the real pleasures has been working with the White House staff. I am sure you can't find a better group of men anywhere. Just the other day I called George Reedy on the phone and asked him what time the dinner for the Princess of Luxembourg was.

"He said, 'I am sorry, I don't know about any dinner.'

" 'But, George, you announced it to the press at Monday's briefing.'

" 'I don't remember *having* a briefing on Monday,' he said.

" 'George,' I said, 'there *is* a dinner tonight for the Princess of Luxembourg.'

" 'I don't have any information on that. I will have to check it out.'

" 'George,' I said, 'do you know who you are talking to?' [Pause.]

" 'I'm not sure.'

" 'This is the Vice-President of the United States.' [Long pause.]

"He said, 'Could you give me a few more details.'

"Now, of course, this meeting is strictly off the record. Nothing ever gets printed from the Gridiron Dinner. So I know there isn't the *slightest* chance it will *ever* get back to the President [pause] that I have my own ideas . . . [Pause] my own visions of what the Great Society might encompass.

"I see, for example, a society in which reporters get paid like publishers, and publishers think and vote like reporters. I see an America in which Harry Byrd is as liberal as Wayne Morse—and Wayne talks as little as Byrd.

"I see a world in which Maxwell Taylor writes a syndicated column—and General Joseph Alsop runs the war in Vietnam . . . a world in which General de Gaulle lets England into the Common Market—and the United States lets General de Gaulle into Fort Knox—just to advise it.

"I see a world in which Nikita Khrushchev comes *out of* retirement and Dick Nixon goes in.

"Gentlemen, there are no bounds to my visions of America, my optimism, my belief in its future. I see a day when extremism in the defense of the Great Society is no vice and moderation in the pursuit of Republicans is no virtue."

⟮ After Humphrey's nomination as Democratic Vice-Presidential candidate, Lyndon Johnson invited him to spend a weekend at the LBJ Ranch. During the visit the President summoned Hubert for a parley in the cow pasture, whereupon Humphrey promptly stepped in some cow dung. "Mr. President," declared Hubert, regaining his equanimity and his balance, "I just stepped on the Republican platform!"

❲ As Humphrey was waiting in the rose garden for President Johnson to summon him into his office, a light rain began to fall. Taking note of this fact, one of the reporters present suggested that they move to some cover. Humphrey retorted with a grin, "Oh, is it raining? I thought we were being blessed."

❲ Cautious politicians do not declare their intentions to run for the office of Vice-President. Rather, they discreetly keep themselves "available" by courting the "right friends" and holding frequent interviews. During the summer of 1964, Hubert Humphrey kidded about this political ritual. "Just look at what's happened. The President sent Bobby Kennedy to the Far East. He sent Sargent Shriver to deliver a message to the Pope. Adlai Stevenson got to escort Mrs. Johnson when she went to the theater in New York. So I asked the President 'who's going to enroll Lynda Bird in George Washington University? I'll volunteer.' "

❲ With characteristic irony, Hubert Humphrey comments upon his momentous choice to accept the Vice-Presidential candidacy in the 1964 election:

"I weighed the decision on the Vice-Presidency very carefully. Not long but carefully." Humphrey was unsure as to what qualities he possessed for the office, "but I know one that I didn't have . . . reluctance!"

❲ In 1965, Vice-President Humphrey reported on a bit of research he had done on his predecessors and their contributions to the office. "Who can forget those storied Vice-Presidents of the past?" he cried. "William A. Wheeler! Daniel D. Thompkins! Garret A. Hobart! and Henry Wilson!"

⟨ Audiences along Humphrey's 1964 campaign route heard him declare that he had breakfast once a week in the White House, adding, "Of course, it's no secret that, four years ago, I had hoped of having breakfast at the White House *every* morning."

⟨ Vice-President Hubert Humphrey can not only take a good joke, but can also tell one on himself. In regard to the perennial view of the Vice-Presidency as little more than a collection of odd jobs, Humphrey told a group of returning Peace Corps veterans in 1965, "You've talked about your frustrations," and added, "you know the Vice-President doesn't have much to do—historically. You know those big meetings over at the White House, and then somebody looks around and says, 'What's left over? Where's Hubert?'" The prevailing myth is that if the President had his way, it soon will be, "Hubert who?"

⟨ In April, 1964, Hubert Humphrey spoke of his political aspirations: "I'm like the girl next door—always available but you don't necessarily think about marriage."

⟨ Shortly after leaving the Senate to assume the Vice-Presidency in 1965, Humphrey said of his new post, "I like it, why not? The working conditions are good. The pay is better."

⟨ Attending a dinner with Hubert Humphrey, famed entertainer Rosalind Russell was discussing the burdens of public office. Miss Russell noted that the Presidency must be the most difficult office in the world, but Humphrey asserted that the Vice-Presidency was harder. "The President has only 190 million bosses," he explained, "The Vice-President has 190 million *and one.*"

❲ Vice-President Humphrey relates this story of the origin of the ornate chandelier adorning his Senate office:

"That chandelier used to hang in the White House, but it kept President Theodore Roosevelt awake. Teddy Roosevelt was supposed to be a big brawny guy, a Rough Rider, but he suffered from insomnia. And in those days," explained Humphrey, "without air conditioning, the White House windows were wide open at night, and the wind hitting that chandelier made it tinkle.

"Finally Teddy told his wife, 'Send that chandelier up to the Vice-President's office where it can keep him awake.' In those days," adds the busy Vice-President parenthetically, "the Vice-President had nothing much to do."

❲ During 1965, when there was considerable speculation about an "official residence" for the Vice-President, Hubert Humphrey, attending a party in Chevy Chase, announced, "We love our neighbors. Despite anything you read in the paper, I am content where I am. I will be content here until 1968 and even until 1972. I don't know if Vice-Presidents can run for a third term but if they can, I'll be content with that too."

❲ In January, 1966, Vice-President Humphrey sent a message all the way from Asia to the annual dinner of the Women's National Press Club. The note began, "Friends and armchair Vice-Presidents, greetings from Prime Minister Kosygin."

Humphrey went on to say that the query "Whatever happened to Hubert Humphrey?" never bothered him, since he had been occupied with a number of things, among them reading some of his favorite poetry:

"Lives of statesmen all remind us
As their pages o'er we turn
That we shouldn't leave behind us
Memos someone ought to burn."

In return, the Vice-President asked, "Whatever happened to the press?" He reported working longer hours on space, on civil rights, and on the President's legislative program, but, he wondered, "Where are you?" Humphrey predicted that if the press corps continues to diminish at its present rate, there will be no radio, TV, or newspapers by 1972.

⟨ Addressing the nation's political scientists in September, 1965, Vice-President Hubert Humphrey disclosed that when he was a vice-president of the American Political Science Association, "No one suggested elevating me to the Presidency. Now I hope that doesn't get out of this room."

"Of course," he quickly added, "that was a long time ago and now everybody writes about how Humphrey has changed."

⟨ Appearing before a national television audience in January, 1966, Humphrey good-naturedly poked fun at himself and at one of Madison Avenue's most cherished clichés:

AGRONSKY: "How do you feel about your Vice-Presidential image?"

HUMPHREY: "Well, it is fourteen-and-a-half pounds lighter than it was, let me say, about three months ago."

◖ "There have been many things related about the status of the Vice-Presidency," states Humphrey. "I thought you'd like to know that I enjoy it. I tell the President that every day, too."

◖ The intimation that Lyndon Johnson might have worried that Humphrey would somehow upstage him in the 1964 Presidential campaign was lightly ridiculed by the Vice-President, who observed, "That's like Rembrandt worrying about a college art student."

◖ In 1964, shortly before President Johnson finally selected Hubert Humphrey as his election running mate, the President was breakfasting with several Congressional leaders. As he lifted his glass of orange juice to his lips, he suddenly burst into laughter. Across the table, wearing a mischievous grin, sat Humphrey. Under the President's juice glass lay a Johnson-Humphrey campaign button, clipped from the cover of a national magazine and placed there by the future Vice-President.

◖ An exchange overheard between Humphrey and Lyndon Johnson:
    LBJ: "Where did you get that good-looking jacket?"
    HHH (pretending to examine the label of his sportscoat): "It says here, 'Neiman-Marcus, courtesy of Billie Sol Estes.'"

◖ The President always expected leaders of Congress to be readily available by telephone and accordingly ribbed the then-Senator Humphrey at one legislative breakfast in

1964, "I tried to get hold of you yesterday. Where were you?" Replied Humphrey, turning his head and smiling benignly, "Try the other cheek, Mr. President."

❡ President Johnson kept everyone in the dark about his choice of a running mate for the 1964 elections. Humphrey was presumed to be high on the list of possibilities, but the President enjoyed teasing him by consulting him about other Vice-Presidential choices. Noted Humphrey, "He discussed every move and thought with me as if nothing could interest me less personally. It's like a guy calling the girl next door—who he knows is madly in love with him—to ask the phone number of the newest broad in town."

❡ At the commencement exercises for Syracuse University's Class of 1965, Humphrey was presented with a gold tieclasp in the shape of a Phi Beta Kappa key. "I shall wear it," said Humphrey, "but you don't think Lyndon Johnson will be sore if I take his off?"

❡ Appearing twenty minutes late for an address he was to make before a 1965 meeting of NATO parliamentarians, Hubert Humphrey explained, "It took thirty-six minutes to fly from Washington to La Guardia Field, and forty-two minutes—with a police escort—to drive in from the airport to this hotel." He then added this plea: "I trust such contradictions will not hamper your efforts toward building a better world."

❡ Vice-President Humphrey was the guest of honor at a reception for 500 delegates to the 1966 Conference of the

National Association of County Officials and their wives. Before addressing the group, he apologized for the absence of his own wife. "I lost Mrs. Humphrey in New York yesterday," he said. "To turn a wife loose in New York without a deadline is a dangerous thing," said the Vice-President. "She was fully armed," he added. "She had her credit card and checkbook with her."

❨ Vice-President Humphrey tells this interesting anecdote about the small mirror that hangs over the grandfather clock in his office. "That came from Dolley Madison. She was a young, good-looking gal, kind of like Jackie Kennedy, who set the town on its ear. She got tired of living in the White House and having it look like an old barn, and decided to decorate it. She went to Europe and bought that mirror for forty dollars. But when she got back to New York, the customs collector wanted to charge her thirteen dollars duty.

"Dolley said, 'To heck with that, this is for the White House; it's not for me.'

"But the customs collector said, 'It doesn't make any difference who it's for, you have to pay thirteen dollars.'

" 'You know what you can do with it,' Dolley said, and she left it in New York. When she got back to Washington, she told her husband, the President, about it. 'Jim,' she said, 'I want that collector fired.' President Madison fired him.

"Then the Congress investigated," said Humphrey, "spent about a year investigating, and wrote a big, thick report called 'The Dolley Madison Mirror.' It cost $2,000 to conduct that investigation, after which Congress demanded that President Madison rehire the customs collector. Madison refused. And out of that came the very important doctrine of the separation of the Executive and the Congress.

"President Madison told Congress, 'You can tell me what kind of a man to hire, whether he should be fat or thin or what kind of qualifications he should have, but you can't tell me who to hire. That's up to me.'

"The Congress also found that no matter who you are, you have to pay customs. Even if you're the wife of the President or the wife of a Congressman, you have to pay. There must be equality.

"So," said the Vice-President, "for that $2,000, the cost of the investigation, we got two important doctrines for the American Government—the separation of the Executive and Congress, and the equality of all people when it comes to taxes and tariffs."

❲ Vice-President Humphrey has always loved to talk and often finds himself incapable of stopping himself. As a senator he frequently filled large segments of the Congressional Record when the legislature was in session. Once, while repeating the old rhetorical formula "Mr. President, I ask permission to insert in the Record . . . ," he slipped and said, "I ask permission to insert in my Record . . ."

❲ In vividly describing a heated Senate debate, Hubert Humphrey once astounded guests at a diplomatic dinner at the British Embassy by announcing, "Oh, boy, and then did the manure hit the fan!"

❲ Speaking before the National Association of Retail Druggists in 1962, Hubert Humphrey twitted his own well-known propensity to talk. "I told a few folks who do not know me very well, 'I'll speak about twenty or twenty-five minutes.' And then I told my good friends, 'I will perhaps make it about an hour.' I never let my friends down."

⟨[The Vice-President willingly admits that he is a "compulsive talker, the way an alcoholic drinks."

⟨[In the 1960 Wisconsin Presidential primary, the Kennedy family, including John, Bobby, Ted, and often their mother and sisters, frequently contributed to Jack's campaign with speeches, handshaking, and the like. Noted Humphrey, "I feel like an independent merchant competing against a chain store."

⟨[The 1960 Democratic Convention over, Humphrey turned to patching up intraparty squabbles and to campaigning for John F. Kennedy. "I want to say one thing about Senator Kennedy. If he gives you his word and says he is going to do it, he does it. He told me last year that he was going to lick me, and he did it."

⟨[In Australia Humphrey was greeted with some boos from demonstrators protesting American policies. The Vice-President, attending a luncheon, cracked that Prime Minister Holt would do anything "to make me feel at home," even to providing the customary demonstration, although not one "as large as we can produce."

⟨[During the Presidential campaign in 1964, Hubert Humphrey made this reference to the Republican nominee's reputedly negativistic attitudes: "And where was Senator Goldwater? He was under the no-no tree in the shadow of his own indifference."

⟨[The driver of a car carrying Hubert Humphrey to an appointment for which he was late attempted to regain lost time by speeding. Nervously, the Vice-President cautioned him to slow down: "I'd rather be the Hubert Humphrey who came late than the late Hubert Humphrey."

⟨[As Humphrey was conducting a 1964 campaign rally, a small group of Goldwater rooters began the chant "We want Barry," to which Hubert replied, "OK, which will it be, raspbarry or strawbarry?"

⟨[Humphrey, scheduled to speak before the March, 1963, dinner of the Gridiron Club, was called by President Kennedy, who wanted to know what he was going to say in his address. "Well," replied Humphrey, "I almost hesitate to tell you, Mr. President. I'm writing the speech now and I am thinking of putting in a paragraph ribbing Nelson Rockefeller that will read something like this: 'Gentlemen, the American people would never tolerate a President who might appoint his brother Winthrop to head the Peace Corps, his brother Laurance to a Cabinet position, and let his brother David run for the Senate. This nation would not permit a dynasty.' "

⟨[Speaking before the Football Writers Association of America in 1965, Vice-President Humphrey began, "Well, I want to say a word or two about this all-star game and about football in general. I am going to speak with a great deal of insight and erudition about football because I know so little about it. Some of the best speeches I have made have been in that vein, so if you will just sort of lean back, I would like to share with you a few pertinent observations from an impertinent person."

Later, referring to his favorite home-state baseball team, the Vice-President said, "This year, I haven't done a thing to help the Twins. I haven't even bought a ticket. I have attended a couple of games, but I never bought any tickets, and they are way out front. Cal Griffith said to me the other day, 'Mr. Vice-President, as a spectator you are great, but please stop trying to make policy.' So I know now where I stand."

(When President John F. Kennedy returned from his trip to Ireland, bursting with stories of his marvelous reception there, Humphrey had this to say: "Mr. President, while you were off seeing your relatives in Ireland, I was back home in Minnesota. The Chippewa Indians made me a chief. I am Chief Leading Father. And what's more, Mr. President, *they* all have votes."

(Just before the November, 1964, Presidential election, in response to Barry Goldwater's accusing President Johnson of "daddyism," Humphrey declared, "He's against daddy, against labor, and against old people and young people. And there's still time for him to say something against mother."

(Senator Hubert Humphrey discussed one segment of his famed eight-hour talk with Khrushchev in Moscow:

K: "We are having trouble testing our intercontinental ballistic missiles. They shoot too far. . . . You Americans . . . have lots of space to shoot your rockets. . . ."

HHH: "Well, if you are having all this trouble, we will be glad to test your rockets for you."

⟨ As an eager freshman senator, Humphrey once asked advice from a more experienced colleague: "Be sure to brief me on protocol. I'm liable to start sliding down the bannister."

⟨ As Vice-President Humphrey was leaving South Vietnam on his 1966 Southeast Asian tour, Chief of State Nguyen Can Thieu invited him to return and hunt an elephant some time. Responded Humphrey, "I spend most of my time at home hunting elephants."

⟨ A group of students once asked Humphrey how a supposed "liberal" could oppose a bill to allow the coloring of oleomargarine. Explained the Senator with a grin, "I counted up the dairy farmers in Minnesota and the oleo manufacturers. There were more dairy farmers."

⟨ In Waverly, Minnesota, Hubert Humphrey is fond of driving around in a Model A Ford that had cost $2,000. In retaliation his wife has purchased an old Kimball player piano. Their son Douglas commented that perhaps the piano was the better bargain, whereupon Hubert advised him, "Son, make a value judgment. Could you get more dates with that piano or my Ford?"

❰ During his 1954 campaign to retain his Senate seat in Minnesota, Humphrey was criticized for his membership in Americans for Democratic Action, a group allying itself with liberal forces. Asked by a reporter how, as an officer of the ADA, he met this challenge by his constituent farmers, Hubert replied, "I simply declare to them in answer that things had come to a sad pass when a man could be so abused for belonging to that fine old American institution the American Dairyman's Association."

❰ Just prior to the taping of a national television interview in 1962, a network executive advised Humphrey to relax, to imagine that he was speaking to a friend of average intelligence, education, and income. "That's fine," Humphrey replied, "but what about the unfriendly people, the dumb ones, the geniuses, the plumbers, the philosophers, the slum dwellers, and the fat cats in the audience?"

❰ Humphrey is responsible for dubbing the Communist scheme for world domination "Operation Nibble."

❰ Quipped Humphrey to a group of student supporters of Barry Goldwater during the 1964 campaign, "I don't care if you study ancient history, but don't *vote* for it."

❰ Hubert Humphrey displayed the same wit as Senator that he does as Vice-President. This selection from the debate on the McCarran Immigration Bill in 1952 shows Humphrey at his humorous best:

HUMPHREY OF MINNESOTA: "Do I understand correctly that under the terms of the bill the Attorney General is to have something to say about whether or not a marriage relationship has been fulfilled and is satisfactory? That certainly smacks of something new in legislation."

MOODY OF CALIFORNIA: "It certainly smacks of something. The bill provides that if a bride and bridegroom come into this country under a marriage relationship and fail to fulfill the marital agreement to the satisfaction of the Attorney General . . ."

HUMPHREY: "Just a moment. Let us stop there."

MOODY: "I do not know why the Attorney General should be interested in that, but perhaps he is."

HUMPHREY: "I do not believe Congress should put the burden upon the Attorney General as to whether a marriage relationship is satisfactory or has been properly consummated."

MOODY: "That is my point."

HUMPHREY: "What is the express language of the bill?"

MOODY: " 'Failure to fulfill marital agreements to the satisfaction of the Attorney General.' "

HUMPHREY: "'I think we should ascertain from the sponsors of the bill just what that means. It sounds very interesting."

MOODY: "It would be interesting to know."

HUMPHREY: "The Attorney General is going to be a very busy man under this bill. Not only that, he is going to be in on some secrets he ought not to be in on."

PASTORE OF RHODE ISLAND: "As a matter of fact the McCarran Bill may become the best seller of the year."

HUMPHREY: "It will certainly become a sort of Kinsey report."

⟨ After his defeat by John Kennedy in the 1960 West Virginia primary, Hubert Humphrey noted that he had done fairly well for a Protestant, and he added, "It isn't impossible for a little man to defeat a big man. After all, David slew Goliath. Of course, what was sufficiently unusual was that 3,000 years later people are still talking about it."

⟨ Hubert Humphrey's transoceanic message to the 1966 Women's National Press Club dinner asserted that the Vice-President would definitely not seek the Senate seat of Leverett Saltonstall of Massachusetts. "Although I feel sincerely I could do more for Massachusetts—and despite my long association with that state—I feel it should be left open there for the young people of the Democratic Party who have worked their way up to this opportunity."

⟨ During the fall of 1964, all the Presidential and Vice-Presidential candidates released personal financial reports. Hubert Humphrey's assets were reasonably large, but were dwarfed by those of the other nominees. However, philosophized Humphrey, "There'll be enough to take care of Mother."

⟨ Says Vice-President Humphrey of his spouse, "I married Muriel for her money. She had managed to save up $600 during the Depression years."

⟨ Speaking before the National Association of Retail Druggists in September, 1962, Hubert Humphrey confessed, "I would like to be able to tell you good folks that whatever you want done I can get done for you. I have used that once in a while, but I do not try to use it too often because they catch up with me. . . . If you ever want to see a group of independent men and independent-minded men, just meet a group of Senators. Somebody said, 'Who is the leader of the Senate?' I said, 'Just ask anyone, he will tell you we have one hundred chiefs, one hundred generals—we are a little short on troops.' "

❨ During the oath-taking ceremonies at his inauguration as Vice-President in 1964, Hubert Humphrey doffed his overcoat despite the chilly January weather. Asked if he weren't apprehensive of catching a cold, the ex-pharmacist smiled and replied, "Oh, no. Modern medicine and pharmacy will take care of that."

❨ Stumping in Tifton, Georgia, during the 1964 campaign tour, Vice-Presidential candidate Hubert Humphrey held up a huge Georgia "goober" and proclaimed, "I want to tell you that Lyndon Johnson and Hubert Humphrey like peanuts enough to make the peanut economy worth more than just peanuts."

❨ Vice-President Hubert Humphrey still likes to regard himself as a small-town boy from a "typical American community." Notes Humphrey, "That's pretty conservative country I come from. We still whistle the 'Washington Post March' out there. We don't go in for these far-out things. We don't like far-out art—or far-out politics."

❨ Unable to be patient with governmental inaction or hesitancy, Hubert Humphrey quips, "Most areas of the world suffer from some disease. In many regions it's dysentery. In Washington the disease of the Potomac is timidity."

❪ In November, 1964, Republican Vice-Presidential nominee Bill Miller kidded Democratic counterpart Humphrey about his middle name. Replied Hubert, "I think America is entitled to a Vice-President with the middle name of Horatio."

❪ Before the AFL-CIO Building and Construction Trades Department in 1960, the then-Senator Hubert Humphrey proudly announced, "Out of 214 votes tabulated by the AFL-CIO, I agreed with you 213 times. That's 99.5 per cent purer than Ivory Soap."

❪ Arriving for a campaign stop at Fargo, North Dakota, in October, 1964, Hubert Humphrey strode down his plane's ramp and told the crowd, "I couldn't believe my eyes when I saw this huge crowd so late at night. For a moment I felt like a Republican. I thought I was walking in my sleep."

❪ Hubert Humphrey gives the following short explanation of his celebrated loquacity: "It's just glands."

❪ Democratic candidate Karl Rolvaag won a "squeaker" over Republican Governor Elmer Andersen in Minnesota's gubernatorial race in 1962. The then-Senator Hubert Humphrey compared Rolvaag's 91-vote verdict with President Johnson's famous 87-vote victory over Coke Stevenson in the 1948 Texas primary. "We call Karl 'Landslide' Rolvaag," quipped Humphrey. "That's an honor we once reserved only for Lyndon. I told Rolvaag he ought to be proud of it. He piled up four more votes than the former champion."

❡ During 1960 Senator Hubert Humphrey was expressing his desire for a greater Democratic majority in the Senate when Norris Cotton of New Hampshire interjected for the Republicans:

COTTON: "I am wondering how many [Senators] the Democrats need for a working majority. Today, they have sixty-six members of the Senate. . . . I am confident the distinguished and fine Senator from Minnesota and all his colleagues will do [one thing]. They will see to it that at least we keep one or two Republicans in the Senate."

HUMPHREY: "Yes."

COTTON: "Because so long as there is one Republican among the one hundred Senators, they will have someone on whom to blame everything that happens so that they can capitalize on it with the people. I only hope the Senator from Minnesota loves me so much that he will let me be the one Republican."

HUMPHREY: "Let me say to my good friend from New Hampshire that my affection for him is so sincere that I would be glad to keep him as the one Republican for all to see. In fact, I think we need two Republicans—one in the Smithsonian [Institution] and one here in the Senate."

3 . *The Republican Wits*

❨ LEST THE TITLE of this chapter mislead the reader, it should be stated here that there is no such thing as *the* Republican wit. That is, no particular kind of sense of humor distinguishes a Republican from a Democrat. More often than not, true wit knows no party boundaries. This section collects the assorted speeches, jokes, and gibes of the elected legislators of the Grand Old Party. Although the current (1966) Congress' Democrats outnumber Republicans two to one, it will be seen that the minority party makes up for its deficiency in numbers with a proficiency and an abundance of wit.

It may also be noticed that among the Republican wits are several figures who no longer take an active part in the conduct of government affairs. Their inclusion, however, justifiably reflects the important role they have played in our government and continue to play in the affairs of their party.

⟨ In 1959 the Senate was filled with allegations of national insecurity and undermined defenses. Illinois' Everett Dirksen reached back into his abundant store of Abe Lincoln stories as he spoke in opposition to the charges.

⟨ DIRKSEN: "Mr. President, the distinguished Senator from Missouri [Stuart Symington] stated as follows:

> Mr. President, the American people are being enticed down the trail of insecurity by the issuance of misinformation about our deterrent power; and specifically about the missile gap.
> The intelligence books have been juggled so the budget books may be balanced.
> This is a serious accusation, which I make with all gravity.

"Mr. President, as I take thought of the unending comment in this security field, I think of an old Missourian in the Civil War days who was passionately devoted to the candidacy of John C. Frémont. This old citizen of Missouri was quoted by the Chicago *Times* of that day in a comment which he made about Abraham Lincoln, the Commander in Chief. In that comment he said that Abraham Lincoln's head was 'too light for the weight of his feet.' Then he made a comment on conducting the war, and he said that running the war reminded him a good deal of the manner of a man who was climbing trees to catch woodpeckers. Some friend said, 'You will never catch any woodpeckers that way.' 'Well,' he said, 'maybe not, but if I don't catch 'em I'll worry 'em like hell.'

"I apologize for the term, but it is an exact quote and I got it from the writings of Carl Sandburg.

"It seems to me that in this security field all the comments which are being made are nibbling comments on the sniping side, and disparaging, it seems to me, of the defense effort of this administration.

"When I think of all the comments by persons who seem to think they are better able to do this job in the defense field than is the President of the United States, I think of the Committee on the Conduct of the War, which was established away back in the Civil War days. I make no exceptions. I have in mind Republicans as well as Democrats. On that committee there was a man named Benjamin Wade, from Ohio. He started out as a canal driver and as a mule skinner. Then he became a teacher, as I recall, and then a lawyer. That qualified him to conduct a war. He marched down to the White House, shook his finger at Lincoln, and said, 'You have to fire General McClellan.' Lincoln said, 'Well, whom shall I use to replace him?' And Wade said, 'Anybody.' Lincoln, out of his majestic concepts, said, 'I cannot fight a war with anybody; I must have somebody.'

"Away back in those days we had a little of the same attitude which is now apparent."

⟨ Senator Wayne Morse of Oregon was one of a group who were filibustering against a communications-satellite bill. During the debate, Morse became embroiled with the Democratic Senator Kerr of Oklahoma, and the words became heavily tinged with biting sarcasm. At this point, Republican Senator Everett Dirksen of Illinois broke in: "With respect to the observation of the distinguished Senator from Oregon anent the Senator from Oklahoma, there are people who deem themselves infallible half the time and never wrong the other half."

Suddenly, Senator Ralph Yarborough of Texas stood and announced, inexplicably, that he desired "to read an extract from a letter that was written less than one week before the vote in the Andrew Johnson impeachment proceedings."

Completely unmoved, Dirksen rejoined, "Why go back that far? . . . Mr. President, I do not know what impeachments have to do with satellites. I do not know why we have to go back to 1867. That reminds me of a story. A man went into a restaurant, sat down, and asked, 'What kind of soup do you have?' The waiter replied, 'Oxtail.' The customer said, 'Oh, why go back that far?' "

❨ As Vice-President-elect Hubert Humphrey took over his duties as president of the Senate in January, 1965, Illinois Republican Everett Dirksen rose to welcome him:

"Perhaps I had better address the distinguished majority leader.

"Only a few days ago it was my privilege to present the distinguished Vice-President-elect to a national convention at the Statler Hotel. I was advised that I might begin my speech, and that I would be interrupted when he arrived. The signal was to be that the chairman would pull my coattails to announce the fact that the Vice-President-elect had arrived.

"When he appeared, I looked at his audience and said, 'Ladies and gentlemen, permit me to split an infinitive and let a participle hang from the air for a moment while I present the distinguished Vice-President-elect of the United States.'

"His good fortune has been our good fortune. By electing him to office, we have now shorn him of a good deal of authority. His principal function now will be to break a tie—if ever there is a tie in a body having a ratio of 2 to 1.

"But we have now shorn him of any authority to discuss, with his eloquence and persuasion, the many items that will cross his desk.

"Mr. Vice- President, we are honored. We glory in your good fortune; we glory in our good fortune; and we think we ought to give you a hand. [Applause, Senators rising.]"

❬ In 1965 Senator Everett Dirksen proposed a constitutional amendment in response to a 1964 Supreme Court ruling requiring the reapportionment of both branches of state legislatures. The debate over his amendment elicited this comment from the Illinois Republican: "The time will come when the only people interested in state boundaries will be Rand McNally."

❬ Republican Senator Everett Dirksen admitted at a Women's National Press Club dinner that he had been intrigued by President Johnson's 1966 State of the Union address, and then took note of the absence of the Vice-President. "Hubert doesn't know what he missed! It was the shortest tax cut in history. I love Hubert, I really do—ADA and all."

❬ Speaking before the 1966 Women's National Press Club dinner, Dirksen noted—not without some pride—that in every comparison or contest he has been listed as the worst-dressed man in the country, and that he has been described as looking like "an unmade bed." He felt that perhaps the only thing to be done for the beautification of Congress would be the establishment of beauty shops. "I have been trying for the past two years to get a blue rinse but I haven't yet. If I don't get a blue rinse soon there's going to be no appropriation for the Senate barbershop."

⟨[Dirksen once rocked the Senate back on its heels with this announcement: "I have a surprise for you. I shall depart from my usual custom and talk about the bill that is up for discussion today."

⟨[In 1966 Illinois Senator Everett Dirksen was asked his opinion of the proposal to limit to a single quart the amount of liquor American travelers may bring into the United States from foreign countries. Dirksen quickly responded, "I'd make it a pint. We have a big distillery industry in my state, and it pays a million dollars a day in revenue tax."

"But Ev," the interviewer continued, "foreign countries don't have pints."

"Then let them buy pint bottles from us," Dirksen said. "We also have a big glass industry in Illinois."

⟨[Asked in 1962 if he were offended by the use of the name "Ev and Charlie Show" for his television press conferences, Senator Everett Dirksen answered that the term was as natural as "Corned beef and cabbage, the Cherry Sisters, and Gallagher and Shean."

⟨[In October, 1965, members of the White House press corps threw an unprecedented farewell party for Lawrence O'Brien, who was leaving his position at the White House to assume the Postmaster Generalship. Attending the celebration was Senate minority leader Everett Dirksen of Illinois, who gloated that O'Brien owed him several "favors" for legislative assistance.

"I'm going to coddle O'Brien," Dirksen said. "I'm going to feast O'Brien. I'm going to genuflect even if I am a 33d-degree Mason . . . because frankly I need a lot of brick and mortar back in Illinois."

The Senator also kidded O'Brien about a plan the Republicans had for using commemorative stamps, which can be issued at the discretion of the Postmaster General, as political weapons. "I've got a list," said Dirksen. "You can issue a California stamp that says, 'Ronald Reagan with Love and Kisses'—or in Colorado, where Senator Gordon Allott is up for reelection, you could have something like 'A Ballot for Allott'—and for Douglas in Illinois, you could just say, 'Douglas—Paul, that is, not Stephen A.'"

(In contemplating the issue of which direction—left or right—this generation will take, Illinois Senator Dirksen recalls "the days when circuit judges rode about on horseback. I am advised that down in Kentucky in those days when Abraham Lincoln was a member of the Illinois legislature, they had a judge who had a great fondness for corn liquor.

"One day, when the judge was 'slightly mellow,' he went out to throw a saddle on his horse. A young lawyer watching the operation noticed that the judge had the pommel where the cantle should be. He said, 'Your Honor, you have your saddle on backward!'

"Then, with that kind of dignity that only the judiciary can assume, the judge said, 'How in the devil do you know in what direction I am going?'"

(Notes Senator Everett Dirksen, "During a political campaign, everyone is concerned with what a candidate will do on this or that question if he is elected, except the candidate; he's too busy wondering what he'll do if he isn't elected."

⟨ Illinois Senator Everett Dirksen has a novel way of dealing with especially unfavorable criticism. He cuts the offending matter out of the newspaper and puts the clipping into his pocket. Later, at a meeting or rally, the eloquent Senator warms up his audience to an enthusiastic pitch and then introduces the topic of unfair criticism and how such injustice often deters public officials from serving their constituents.

He then begins to read the most offensive part of the clipping to the sympathetic audience. Suddenly, in the middle of a sentence, Dirksen stops, and feigning utter outrage, splutters, "Oh, my soul! Do you know whom they're talking about? They're talking about me!"

⟨ Senator Everett Dirksen of Illinois was discussing the "gold cover" bill with former Treasury Secretary Douglas Dillon in 1965. He recalled the story of Salmon P. Chase, Abraham Lincoln's Secretary of the Treasury, who once issued a quantity of greenbacks for which there was no gold backing. Chase conferred with Lincoln as to the appropriate inscription for the new issue, and Lincoln finally offered, "Put on it what the Apostle Peter said: 'Silver and gold have I none, but such as I have I give thee.' "

⟨ Republican Senator Everett Dirksen, on Democratic Senator Mike Mansfield, September, 1961: "So the distinguished majority leader, the Senator from Montana [Mansfield], must have, on occasion, philosophized to himself, when he was down in the depths of the earth, either as a miner or as a mining engineer, because there the whole formation of what we see as the planet on which we live must have been unfolded in perspective, and surely must have said to him, 'Take your time. Take your time.' So he has accomplished a great work without unseemly or undue haste.

"He reminds me a little of the old grandfather clock. If one thinks of the modern alarm clock, as distinguished from the old grandfather clock, it expresses and articulates the difference in our approaches and in our viewpoints. Perhaps I could describe it best in romantic terms, because in earlier days, when a young man came to court his lady love, he did not come in a Corvair, or a Galaxie, or a Cadillac. He came in an old buggy drawn by a horse, and took his time; and when he got to the home of his lady love, he put the horse in the stable, and then was ushered into the parlor, which was opened only one day a week. It had a fancy lamp on the center table, and a bright red Brussels rug on the floor, and a whatnot on the corner shelf, with all the little knickknacks obtained at a carnival or a state fair. Then he would sit on one end of the horsehair sofa and she on the other. Then there would be that quiet, agonizing, sweating hour after hour as they said exactly nothing. I remember on one occasion, after such an agonizing and excruciating loveliness, a young man blurted out, 'Mary, how's your Maw—not that I give a dern, but just to make conversation?' [Laughter.]

"The old grandfather clock said, 'Take your time, take your time, take your time.'

"It is a little different today. It is symbolized by the alarm clock. The young man comes up in one of the snorting pieces of machinery which we call a convertible, and he plops out, and gets into the parlor. He is not bothered with a rug, unless they want to cut a rug, and take it up and then get down to the business of swinging themselves to one of those boxes with a saxophone player who sounds like a jackass or a drummer from Kansas City who has Saint Vitus's dance. The alarm clock says, 'Get there, get there, get there.'

"As between the old grandfather clock and the alarm clock, MIKE MANSFIELD typifies the old grandfather clock. [Laughter.] 'Take your time, take your time.' How charming and indulgent he has been. He has failed us only two or three times in this session. He vowed that there would be no Saturday sessions. Only twice within my recollection did a Saturday session occur, and I forgive him for the deviation that happened on those two occasions. [Laughter.]"

⟨[Senator Dirksen tells the story of the fellow who witnessed an automobile accident and was called upon to testify at the trial.

Counsel said, "Did you see the accident?"

He said, "Yes, sir."

Counsel asked, "How far were you away when the accident happened?"

He said, "Twenty-two feet nine and three-quarter inches."

Counsel looked at the court and looked at the jury and said, "Well, Smartie, tell the court and jury, how do you know it was twenty-two feet nine and three-quarter inches?"

He said, "When it happened, I took out a tape measure and measured from where I stood to the point of impact, because I knew some lawyer was going to ask me that question."

⟨[During the 1959 Senate debate on budget appropriations, Everett Dirksen argued that information given by the then-Senator Lyndon Johnson told only a part of the story. "The statement made by the majority leader on a number of occasions on the floor and in the tables he inserted in the Record are quite correct so far as they go. As I said before, however, it is like the man who fell off the twentieth floor of a building. As he passed the sixth floor a friend shouted to him, 'Mike, so far you're all right.' "

❬ Advocating a spirit of amity among his Republican and Democratic colleagues on the Senate floor in 1954, Senator Everett Dirksen was reminded of the story of "the two deacons, the Republican and the Democrat, who were kneeling together in their supplications in a little church in a small village in Illinois. The Republican deacon was praying to the Lord and saying, 'O, Lord, make us Republicans unlike the Democrats; make us hang together in accord; make us hang together in concord.' And just then his Democratic brethren [*sic*] said, 'Lord, any cord will do.' "

❬ Dirksen, newly out of sickbed, made this forensic foray on the Senate floor during 1964: "We Republicans are very literal, and frequently, literate people. When we read perfectly plain English we are invariably led into taking it at face value. If we read that capital investment should be encouraged, that consumer purchasing power should be stimulated, that consumers should be protected, or, for example, that higher education should be encouraged, who can censure us—except possibly for our innocence—for believing that any proposals we might make to hasten these ends would not receive White House approval, even active support?

"So perhaps you can imagine my bedridden amazement, my pajama-fuffled consternation, yes, my pill-laden astonishment this week, to learn that three Republican-sponsored proposals to assist in achieving these laudable goals had been defeated by very narrow margins, victims of that new White House telephonic half-Nelson known as the 'Texas twist.'

"To those of you on the Democratic side of the aisle who are still rubbing your bruised arms, I can only extend my sympathy and hope that you who must face the electorate this fall won't need it. To you on the Republican side of the aisle I happily extend my admiration and gratitude for the unanimous support you gave each of the three proposals. When Republicans stand together, without a single defector, on three crucial Senate votes, then the entire nation must know we were right."

⟪ Commented Dirksen in 1961 on President Kennedy's much-publicized rocking chair, "I like rocking chairs. They give you such a sense of motion without any danger."

⟪ Dirksen turned the bright light of his wit on one of the foreign-aid appropriations bills before the Senate in 1964: "The sun has begun to shine through the old oaken door, and the shadow of Santa is falling across the Senate."

⟪ Ev Dirksen philosophizes on the lot of the Congressman: "You must have a rare amount of patience here. You must give no umbrage. You must always try to hear everything the other person says. . . . The oil can is mightier than the sword."

⟪ Illinois Republican Senator Everett Dirksen points out the "ghastly cowardice" of all men in the public eye: "You cannot bear the thought of losing office."

❰ Senator Everett Dirksen is fond of the story about "little Johnny," whose teacher asked him, "How do you spell 'straight'?"

He said, "S-T-R-A-I-G-H-T."

The teacher then asked, "What does it mean?"

Johnny replied, "Without ginger ale."

❰ "Whatever happened to Hubert Humphrey?" was the title of a speech Everett Dirksen was scheduled to deliver early in 1966. Drawled Dirksen in answer, "Well, there was a conjunction of forces that finally brought him to where I always hoped he would be—in a seat of dignity where he can't say a word."

❰ An unmistakable note of pride enters Everett Dirksen's voice as he tells of his ability to dissemble upon the Senate stage. "I have been able to bring a blush to my face, the blush of rage, as I brandished my clenched fist and thrust my face within six inches of the face of another senator during debate on the floor. I was able to relax instantly and smile to show it was a sham. My colleagues seemed to think it was the funniest thing they had ever seen—I looked around and felt they were all near death from apoplexy."

❰ One of the milder vagaries of our foreign-aid policy in 1965 gave Dirksen some pause. "When we sent nineteen tons of bubble gum to Belgium, I saw red. I felt it was a heinous imposition on the American taxpayer. Of course, the voters in downstate Illinois *ate it up* when I told them about those poor, emaciated Belgian kids *mashing* away on that gum and popping the bubbles on their chins."

❨ An eye ailment once took Senator Dirksen to a specialist who, as the Senator recalls, had a very curt manner.

"We shook hands. Then he said, 'Well, let's get on with the business at hand.'

" 'And what is the business at hand?' asked Dirksen, with mounting alarm.

" 'Removing your eye,' said the surgeon, blandly.

" 'Doctor,' said Dirksen, 'on the way here I enlisted the services of another doctor.'

" 'What?' asked the specialist. 'Who?'

" 'The Big Doctor,' said Dirksen.

" 'I don't understand you.'

" 'The Doctor in the sky,' replied Dirksen. 'The Doctor Who watches over us all.'

" 'Indeed?' said the specialist. 'What did He tell you?'

" 'He told me,' said Dirksen, 'to keep my eye.'

" 'Well,' said the surgeon, 'make up your mind. I've got to go out of town.'

" 'I have made it up,' said Dirksen. 'Good-bye, sir.'

"It's my best eye today," said Dirksen, with evident satisfaction.

❨ On November 19, 1965, ex-Senator Barry Goldwater addressed a dinner held in honor of William F. Buckley and the *National Review*, of which Buckley is the editor. The date places the dinner just one year after Goldwater had been defeated in the Presidential elections and only days after Buckley had been defeated in his race for mayor of New York on the Conservative ticket. Here are a few of the remarks that Goldwater prepared for the occasion:

"I'm that trigger-happy s.o.b. you've all read about. But things could be worse. Robert McNamara could be President and I could be Secretary of Defense. . . .

"People ask me if I ever think about the 1964 election

and I have to admit it, I do. Because, in the words of that immortal commercial: 'If they don't put you in the driver's seat—it Hurtz.' . . .

"What can you really say in a city that you lost by 1,387,-021 votes? It's nice to be among friends. Even if they're not yours. . . .

"I always said, if you're going to lose them, lose them big, Bill. . . .

"Running as a Conservative in New York City must be an interesting experience. You're not really a candidate. You are a political kamikaze. . . .

"Actually, Bill didn't really expect to win the election. If I had to define Bill Buckley—I'd say he was a Goldwater who did it on purpose. . . .

"But Bill Buckley ran a great race. I understand at one point, Bobby Kennedy was so worried, he put Staten Island in his wife's name. . . .

"As a candidate for mayor, the editor was apparently unconvincing. As a political kingmaker, he was a 'wrong-way Corrigan!' . . .

"I had an interesting dream last night. The scene was Johnson City, Texas, and Bill Buckley was moving into a brand new house. And across the highway Lyndon was nudging Lady Bird and saying, 'Well, there goes the neighborhood.' . . .

"Bill Buckley, as you know, is the author of *God and Man at Yale*. 'Course, since he wrote it—one of them has gone to the White House. . . .

"It's just a wonder what *National Review* has accomplished. As of October 31 the combined circulation of the *National Review* and the *Reader's Digest* was 22 million copies."

❲ Barry Goldwater tells the story about how "Khrushchev had certain problems. He found that Stalin's memory haunted him and finally he figured the best way to fix that was to get rid of Stalin's body. So he called President Kennedy and asked if he'd take the body. Kennedy explained he didn't want a Communist dead or alive in the United States, but suggested he call Macmillan. Macmillan gave Khrushchev the same line, that he would like to help him but it would cause too much political trouble, and suggested, 'Try de Gaulle. Every once in a while that fellow will help you and besides he enjoys offending the Americans.' Well, de Gaulle explained to Khrushchev that he had trouble at home and abroad, but suggested he try Ben-Gurion: 'There's a little fellow who's pretty decent, and his country has the most relaxed immigration laws. He'll probably help you.' So Khrushchev called Ben-Gurion, told him his dilemma, and said, 'We'll bring the body in the dark of night, absolutely clandestinely and you won't have anything to worry about.' Ben-Gurion answered, 'Oh, Mr. Khrushchev, don't give it a thought. We're tickled to death to help you. Just bring that body down here any time in broad daylight. We'll take care of it. But I have to remind you, Mr. Khrushchev, that my country has the highest rate of resurrection in the world.' "

❲ The Alfalfa Club's mock Presidential candidate for 1962 was Senator Barry Goldwater of Arizona. In his "acceptance speech," the text of which follows, the Republican conservative displays considerable aptitude for political burlesque:

"Mr. President, fellow members of this convention, guests:

"Thank you, Mr. Graham [the late Philip L. Graham, president of the Washington *Post* and *Times Herald*]. Believe me, it is an honor to be nominated by a man of your distinction, and I am very grateful to Herblock [*Post* and *Times Herald* cartoonist] for giving you the evening off to perform this vital task. While seated at the table I turned to my friend and able colleague from Kentucky, Thruston Morton, and remarked that there are a lot of Republicans here tonight and he quickly commented that Republicans cannot afford $100 dinners and settled for this $25 one.

"This is the most exciting thing that has happened to me since [Walter] Reuther made me an honorary Auto Worker. Frankly, I feel that I am long overdue for this nomination. But in my modesty, I can't believe that there are not others better qualified. Personally, I think Nelson Rockefeller would make a wonderful President. Although I don't know how the White House would look with those gas pumps out in front.

"I notice that Mr. Kennedy and his chief scout aren't here tonight and, if someone can carry the word to the President, tell him he would have been in no danger appearing with me tonight—we're not on television. I understand the President and Vice-President are out raising money to pay off the campaign debt. They could each give up one week's allowance and take care of that.

"Now, gentlemen, if my voice trembles a little at this historic moment, I'm sure you will understand. Emotion chokes me when I think that you have chosen a barefoot boy from the Arizona 'valley of fear' to lead this underprivileged, undernourished, underhoused, underclothed and over-Kennedied nation of under 190 million underlings back to the Old Frontier of McKinley's day. The UNDERtaking, naturally, overwhelms me. It takes my breath away even though I feel the White House is ready for me since Jacqueline remodeled it in an eighteenth-century decor, and I feel this is a double honor since I've never even been to Harvard.

"But this has been a genuine draft—not just the kind felt by Reservists—and I have yielded to it in the sincere belief that no man with a drop of patriotism in his veins could turn down such a golden opportunity to advance his family. Of course the Goldwater clan is not as large as the Kennedy clan. And my brother, Bob, doesn't want to be in government—he promised Dad he'd go straight. Besides, somebody has got to mind the store. Which reminds me, I must have the books audited.

"But I have a lot of uncles and cousins and in-laws whom I wouldn't mind shifting to the government payroll. Anything at all—Peace Corps, Justice Department, Senator from Massachusetts—just anything so long as it isn't one of those dollar-a-year jobs. And don't forget, I have a sister named Carolyn and a granddaughter named Carolyn, which I figure puts me two up in that department.

"Since the Attorney General's famous parachute jump from the dome of the Capitol, we now have a three-party system—Republican, Democrat and Teamsters. This opens a whole new vista for elections. Before, the Democrats had to carry away their own ballot boxes. Now the Teamsters can do the job, whether they dump them in the Illinois River or the Rio Grande.

"Which reminds me, I have a grandson who's too young to vote but too old to be Attorney General. This may be an asset.

"Now right at the beginning let me scotch one bit of campaign slander the opposition has come up with. It is perfectly true that, during the heat of the preconvention maneuvering, I said that, if nominated, I would not accept and, if elected, I would not serve. But that statement was lifted out of context and deliberately distorted.

"In the first place, when I said it things didn't look so good. But do they tell you that? Of course not. They claim that I meant it. What I really said was that Sherman had

said it first. Eisenhower had said it in 1948, Adlai had said
it in 1952—and wishes to God he'd stuck to it—and Nixon
is saying it now. It beats me how they can take a clear-cut
sentence like that and distort it. Why, even *Pravda* garbled
it in translation and they usually get things right.

"I will not deny that I've thought about the Presidency.
Somebody ought to think about it. And I'm not afraid of
the Presidency. They say it's the loneliest job in the world.
But those who say it have never been a Republican in this
Senate. Besides, there are many risks to being President—I
saw that President Kennedy was *Time* magazine's 'man of
the year.' Did you see his picture on the cover? I didn't
even know that Everett Dirksen could paint.

"I would not be truthful if I said that I was fully qualified
for the office. I do not play the piano. I seldom play golf,
and I never play touch football. I hope you will find it in
your hearts to accept a President who just sits behind a
desk and works.

"Now, I must take note of the fact that my opponents
call me a conservative. If I understand the word correctly,
it means to 'conserve.' Well, then, I'm just trying to live up
to my name and conserve two things that most need con-
serving in this country—gold and water.

"I don't apologize for being a conservative. I can remember when 'conservative' and 'mother' were clean
words.

"Now let me turn to my campaign platform. As you all
know, I have argued for some time that we should do away
with the cumbersome and lengthy, unmeaningful and
platitudinous promises that the platforms of both parties
have become. We need bold, brief statements that all
Americans can understand.

"With this in mind and hoping to avoid any floor fight
over the platform, I called the two gentlemen who wrote
the 1960 Republican platform and asked the hopeful next

Governor of California to have a midnight meeting with the current and next Governor of New York.

"These things are no good, apparently, unless they are done at the witching hour of midnight.

"Well, that was two weeks ago, and they're still arguing. They have a tentative draft that runs over 1 million words. You see, Dick has just written a book, which he thinks would make a good platform, that runs 500,000 words right there. And, of course, Nelson wants equal time.

"And I gathered that they were both thinking of 1968, so I said, 'The hell with that,' and sat down and wrote a platform with only three planks. I've eliminated all the usual gobbledygook and tried to make it concise and concrete so that everybody will know just where I stand.

"The first plank fits neatly on one page, but I think it's basically sound and honest. It will mean the same thing to you whether you live in the North or the South, whether you're a farmer in Maine or an industrial worker in California. It says, and I ask you to pay close attention: ELECT GOLDWATER.

"That's it. No nonsense, no shilly-shallying, no hairsplitting—just ELECT GOLDWATER. It's got a nice ring to it that I sorta like and is there anyone, from the highest to the lowest, from the ordinary schoolchild to the lowliest Harvard professor, who can possibly mistake this meaning? I'll go even further. Is there anyone in this room who doesn't understand it?

"The other two planks deal with labor, education, foreign policy, and the farm problem. Here's plank No. 2: ELECT GOLDWATER. Now you may notice a certain similarity between the first plank and the second, and I want you to know that that was deliberate. It has been my experience that the public is confused if you offer too many issues. The thing to do is to get hold of one good one and stick to it. Hammer it home. Repetition is the way Madison Avenue sells toothpaste and soap and it's the way the New Frontier stays in the limelight. But when repetition occurs at the White House—and it has since 1932—it's not a sales pitch, it's a giveaway. You don't even have to guess the price.

"And now for the final plank—plank No. 3. This is the bell ringer and it's even shorter. It just says DITTO.

"There you have a campaign platform in five words— ELECT GOLDWATER. ELECT GOLDWATER. DITTO.

"Just to keep things symmetrical, I think I'll hold the budget to five figures. Jayne Mansfield's for openers and I'll accept nominations for the other four.

"Now, no campaign could get rolling without some slogans—words to quicken the patriotic pulses of the people and get them steamed up to go out and elect Goldwater.

"You'll notice that they are set with the compass heading of the New Frontier wagon train and some of them may even strike terror in the heart of Mr. Khrushchev.

"The first one I borrowed from my friend LBJ. It reads: FORGET THE ALAMO.

"Others that are equally inspiring are: SURRENDER, HELL, I HAVE NOT YET BEGUN TO NEGOTIATE.

"Or, MILLIONS FOR DEFENSE. BUT NOT ONE CENT FOR VICTORY.

"And, 54–40, OR A REASONABLE COMPROMISE.

"One more: DAMN THE TORPEDOES—WE'RE UNILATERALLY DISARMED.

"Now, my inaugural address will establish precedent by the same kind of brevity. When I'm sworn in by Earl Warren—who will no doubt regard this act as a violation of his oath of office—all I intend to do is raise my hand and say, 'I do.'

"That's all I said when I was married and it's all I've been able to say around the house ever since. But it's worked out rather well.

"Now, I think you're entitled to know something about the caliber of men I will have in my Cabinet. In presenting the list, I'd like it understood that it is confidential. Also, all the men on this list have promised to respect the priority of their leaks.

"For Secretary of the Treasury, I think I can do no better than to keep Mr. Dillon. Primarily because he has demonstrated that he possesses the one quality so badly needed in these days when we are being pulled one way by the extremists of the left and the other way by extremists of the right. Mr. Dillon is flexible. In fact, you might call him an extreme middle-of-the-roader.

"My hat is off to any man who can argue under Eisenhower that we must beware of the inflationary tug of the mounting national debt and then make a rebuttal under Kennedy by saying a mere 7 billion dollars added to the debt won't hurt us a bit. I believe that Secretary Dillon belongs in Government—I don't think private industry could afford him.

"For Secretary of Defense, I'm sure you'll agree I couldn't do better than Linus Pauling. I figure if we give him three weeks on the job he'll give us a defense without going to the expense of nuclear weapons or bomb shelters, or anything else. That would save us about 60 billion dollars right there and it ain't to be sneezed at.

"Also I rather like his notion of replacing General [Edwin] Walker with Cyrus Eaton. If we're going to indoctrinate the troops, let's do it right.

"Postmaster General is up for grabs. Adlai Stevenson is mad at the Post Office. He couldn't get back the Christmas

card he sent to Nehru. It couldn't be delivered anyway
because Nehru was at a peace conference—that's where he
spends his time between invasions.

"For Secretary of the Interior I certainly would be loyal
to a fellow Arizonian and ask Stew Udall to stay on—I'll
need that oil money anyway. But only if he promises to
stay off Mount Fuji and other people's private property. If
he does a good job, we might even build a statue for him.

"I haven't picked a Secretary of Agriculture yet. I'm
waiting to see what Governors are unemployed.

"As for the State Department, I've been going over their
records and have come to the conclusion we ought to abolish the whole damn thing.

"I don't claim to have all the answers, but, since this
administration took over, I don't even understand the questions.

"And another thing. How is it that our government did
better against General Electric than they did against Cuba?

"I don't want to seem critical. But our first ambassador
in space was a chimp. And so far he's the only one in the
State Department who hasn't made a mistake.

"If I do have a State Department I guess I could keep
Chester Bowles. He's the mystery guest in the Cabinet; in
fact, he's going on *What's My Line?* as soon as he finds out
what his line is. Of course, if the State Department doesn't
work out I can always close it and keep the store open
nights.

"I think it's only fair to tell you I intend to be the President of the whole people and can promise you a nonpartisan administration made up of the best men obtainable. If
there are some good scouts in the New Frontier—and I
have my doubts—I'll ask them to stay even if they have to
be approved by Walter Lippmann.

"For example, I have some definite plans for Professor
Galbraith, Ed Murrow, and Arthur Schlesinger, Jr. I can't

reveal these plans, because if there's a leak they might get out of the country before I'm inaugurated.

"I have some other notions that I shall reserve for my first state-of-the-union message. For example, I'm going to propose a constitutional amendment that any decision of the Supreme Court must make sense. I know it will be controversial, but I think it deserves an airing.

"Further, I will state to the people, 'Ask not what your country can do for you but rather what you can do for your country.' I think I've heard that somewhere. Then I'll ask for a new government agency to study and make recommendations on new things the Government can do for the people. This may take considerable research.

"I think it's time to dust off that old shibboleth 'The people are too damned dumb' and really apply ourselves to the task of taking their property, spending their money, and living their lives for them. It's time they face up to the realities of life and start making some sacrifices.

"The Kennedy Administration has only scratched the surface in this field. Actually, as we mark the first anniversary of the New Frontier, I must say it's been a wonderful year. I wish we could afford it. Now I know why they call it the New Frontier—we're having a harder time crossing it than *Wagon Train*.

"Now, I suppose no acceptance speech would be complete without a reference to the candidate's background. Very simply, I think I'm in the American tradition. I was born in a log cabin, which I had moved to Phoenix, and, except for some air conditioning, a swimming pool, a bowling alley, a bar, a shooting range, and a golf course, it remains the simple log cabin it always was.

"I have nothing against millionaire Presidents. I'd just like to see the day return when people other than Presidents can be millionaires, too.

"I've never hesitated with an answer. When anyone asks

me how I stand on integration, I've only got one answer:
Where are you from?

"Now gentlemen, I have told you the story. The rest is
up to you. Go out and work from now to election day and
fulfill our campaign pledge—ELECT GOLDWATER.
Find more of those districts such as the one the New Frontier turned up in Cook County—the one that had twenty-
two residents but came up with seventy-seven votes. That's
the sort of stuff I mean.

"Gentlemen, I'm flattered that you thought first of my
name. I have every confidence that, with all of you behind
me, I could be another Alf Landon.

"Do your share, and, I pledge you, I will do mine."

(Early in 1966 President Johnson sent Vice-President
Humphrey on a goodwill tour of the Far East and then on
to India to serve as his representative at the funeral of
Prime Minister Shastri. The two trips provoked speculation
that the Administration was attempting to improve the
Vice-President's popularity.

Cracked Barry Goldwater, "Operation Help Hubert.
The most valiant rescue effort since the evacuation of
Dunkirk."

(Barry Goldwater, whose family owns Goldwater's department store in Phoenix, was wearing a tuxedo with
watered-silk lapels in a flowery pattern. "One thing about
owning a store," explained Goldwater, "you've got to wear
the things that don't sell."

(A number of people had recently fallen into the Kennedy family's swimming pool, leading Barry Goldwater to

quip, "When Bobby Kennedy sends out invitations to a formal party, they read, 'Black tie and snorkel.' "

⟨ Vice-President Hubert Humphrey's loquacity is legendary, and Barry Goldwater notes that "Hubert has been clocked at 275 words a minute with gusts up to 340."

⟨ Robert F. Kennedy's chances for the Presidency were being debated even in 1962, at which time Senator Barry Goldwater made this comment: "As of now, I don't think he can be elected President. But, hell, I said that of Jack, too!"

⟨ This was one of Barry Goldwater's contributions to the dialogue concerning Robert Kennedy's activities as Attorney General: "Bobby Kennedy's finally on the right track, I think, about adequate defense. He's in favor of a large standing army—in the South, that is."

⟨ The 1960 campaign gave Barry Goldwater a chance to get in this dig at Lyndon Johnson's disputed television monopoly: "I took off from Dallas this morning, but before I did I asked the lieutenant on the line, 'How do you get to Austin?'

"He said, 'Well, you head south and keep flying about an hour and fifteen minutes and then you're going to see a big city with only one television antenna. That's Austin.' "

⟨ Addressing an Editorial Cartoonists' Convention, Goldwater offered several alternative careers for himself, in the event that the often harshly critical caricaturists of that organization drove him out of politics completely. "The theater kind of appeals to me too. When my contract with Eighteenth-Century Fox runs out I shouldn't have too much trouble. I've been offered the lead in a production called *Stop the World I Want to Get Off*. Also I have been offered a job as consultant on the *Flintstones* TV show. Thanks to some cartoons depicting my political philosophy, the producers got the idea that I am America's foremost authority on the Stone Age."

¶ Barry Goldwater told this story on himself in November, 1965: "I walked across a hotel lobby the other night and I saw these two fellows sitting there. One of them said, 'Hey, look who's over there.'

"And the other fellow said, 'Who is it?'

"And his friend said, 'You don't know who that is? That's Harold Stassen.' "

¶ One of Goldwater's favorite stories concerns the preacher at the first church opened in Tombstone, Arizona. "A tall, bow-legged cowboy approached the minister and said, 'Parson, that was a damn fine sermon.'

" 'Thank you,' replied the preacher, 'but there is no need to use profanity in addressing me.'

"Undaunted, the cowpoke said, 'Yes sir, that was a fine sermon. I liked it so much that I took out my roll and put a hundred dollars on the plate.'

" 'The hell you did,' said the preacher."

¶ Barry Goldwater is fond of relating this story about the Irishman, the Negro, and the Jew who appear at the Gates of Heaven and are granted one wish each by Saint Peter. The Irishman asks for a supply of Irish whiskey to last through eternity. The Negro says that since he has been segregated and mistreated through life, he would like a large white house, a solid gold Cadillac, and two million dollars.

"And when Saint Peter asked the Jew what he wanted, he answered, 'Just give me thirty dollars' worth of costume jewelry and that colored boy's address.'"

❨ This joke is helpful to Barry Goldwater when he is discussing the timeless topic of racial prejudice. Upon landing in the New World, Christopher Columbus approaches two Indians and greets them, "*Cómo está?*" "One Indian turns to the other and says, "This is sure going to play hell with the neighborhood."

❨ When the issue arises over whether there exists any such thing as an "indispensable politician," Goldwater occasionally tells a story about a seven-handed poker game in Phoenix, by way of reply. The members of the game were unreasonably clannish in their behavior, never admitting an outsider to their table. One night, however, one of the players collapsed and died of a heart attack. As they bent over the body, one of the men asked, "What shall we do?"

"Take out the twos and threes, and deal," said another.

❨ Once asked in New York if he were a high or a low Episcopalian, Barry Goldwater responded, "Ask me on a Saturday night."

❨ With a touch of local-color humor, Arizona's Senator Goldwater once expressed his envy of the state of Minnesota for its many lakes. "Out where I come from we have so little water that the trees chase the dogs."

❨ On a wager, Goldwater taught himself to play a tolerable version of "Silent Night" on the trombone. Discussing the future of his musical career, the Arizona Republican indicated a nearby Scottish bagpipe, explaining, "I can't figure out how to hold the doggone thing. It's like making love to an octopus."

❨ Goldwater was once trapped in a broken elevator with several others. A reporter, perusing the elevator's certificates of inspection, cracked, "H'mm, last inspected in 1889."

"That was in my administration," said Goldwater with a grin.

❨ During a speech at Arizona State University in 1965, Barry Goldwater was asked this provocative question from the floor: "If Christ were alive today, would he carry a draft card?" The ex-Senator quickly retorted, "Christ is the only person who wouldn't need a draft card because he'd be the first person to offer his services, not only to his country but to you."

❨ Late in 1965 Barry Goldwater stated the opinion that Secretary of Defense Robert McNamara's policies had reduced Pentagon morale to an all-time low. Cracked the ex-Senator from Arizona, "I would like to see him go back to making Edsels."

❡ In response to a question in 1963 about the sources of his humorous material, Barry Goldwater replied, "I've got ghosts all over the place. I pick up a lot of Fletcher Knebel's stuff too. I sent him an item about Bobby Kennedy's pool, and he sent me two bucks. I sent it right back. I wrote him if we began paying each other off, I'd owe him $2,000 right off the bat."

❡ During a notorious Washington scandal in October, 1964, Barry Goldwater cracked, "As for Bobby Baker, we have a new measure in Washington. It's called the Baker's dozen. They give you thirteen and you kick back two."

❡ During 1963, amateur ham radio operator Barry Goldwater wondered, "What do you suppose the White House would look like with a ten-foot-high ham radio antenna sticking out of the roof?"

❡ At a dinner for editorial cartoonists in May, 1963, Barry Goldwater stated, "I will not be a candidate in 1964. There's too much unemployment now and I'd feel very badly if it fell to my lot to put Vaughn Meader out of work."

❡ Barry Goldwater described President Johnson's State of the Union message of January, 1964: "He has out-Roosevelted Roosevelt, out-Kennedyed Kennedy and . . . made Truman look like [a] piker."

❡ In 1964 Barry Goldwater leveled this sarcastic barb at Michigan's Governor George Romney, then a possible choice for the Republican Presidential nomination: "Governor Romney says he's getting tired of telling people that he's not a candidate for the Republican nomination. What's more, he's getting tired of all the traveling he has to do to tell them."

(En route to Shreveport, Louisiana, aboard a chartered jet, Goldwater's 1964 campaign entourage was shocked to hear the plane's intercom system announce: "This is the captain. Will the stewardess bring up another double martini, please."

It was some minutes before the unsettled passengers could establish that the voice had, indeed, been Goldwater's, not the captain's, and that the Senator was not really drinking martinis in the cockpit, but only embibing a healthy dose of humor.

(Goldwater often displays a facility in using his wit to turn intended barbs back upon the sender, as in the following parry of a gibe by political cartoonist Herbert Block: "I see my friend Herblock has coined a new word in some of his recent cartoons, 'goldbirchers,' and I don't mind telling you that personally I think this is a pretty shabby treatment of Justice Arthur Goldberg."

(During the 1964 Presidential campaign, Barry Goldwater voiced this opinion on the widely discussed topic of the United States educational system: "If we get back to readin', writin', and 'rithmetic and an occasional little whack where it will help, then I think our educational system will take care of itself."

❲ One day during lunch hour, Barry Goldwater's 1964 campaign manager dragged him into a restaurant to shake hands with the customers. Looking embarrassed, Goldwater remarked, "If somebody walked up to me while I was eating lunch and stuck out his hand, I'd put a hamburger right in his palm."

❲ On the campaign trail during 1964, Republican nominee Barry Goldwater stated, "The immediate task before us is to cut the Federal Government down to size . . . we must take Lyndon's credit card away from him."

❲ A favorite 1964 campaign stunt of Barry Goldwater's was to poke a finger through a pair of lensless black-rimmed glasses, saying, "These glasses are just like [Lyndon Johnson's] programs. They look good but they don't work."

❲ Campaigning in Seattle during 1964, Barry Goldwater told the workers at a Boeing bomber plant that had been hard-hit by cutbacks, "I guess when the next war comes, defense officials will go to Hertz rent-a-bomber."

❲ In the peanut-growing state of North Carolina, Barry Goldwater sought votes in the 1964 Presidential election with this message: "I am probably the most violent advocate of peanut butter in history. On a dare from my son, I even shaved with it once, and it was all right, except that it smelled."

⟨ One of Senator Goldwater's campaign slogans for 1964: "LBJ. That stands for Light Bulb Johnson. Let's turn him out in November."

⟨ Commenting with tongue in cheek on his own qualifications for the Presidency, Goldwater noted, "I suppose I might make our finest Civil War President. . . . I'm not sure I have the necessary requirements. My wife gave up fox hunting when I bought her a fur coat—her sister is not a princess—and my brother's too busy minding the store to help me run the show."

⟨ One day in 1964 Barry Goldwater signed off his ham radio broadcast by saying that he had to return to "the Land of Oz—Washington, D.C."

⟨ New York's Senator Keating got the best of this baseball dispute on the Senate floor in 1961:

HUMPHREY: "The senior Senator from North Dakota [Senator Young] some time ago, when Roger Maris had 'belted' a couple of balls out of the ballpark either in New York at the Yankee Stadium, or at some other place, stood upon the floor of the Senate to indicate that Roger Maris was the product of North Dakota. . . . I wish to make the Record clear . . . that Roger Maris is a product of Minnesota. He may have wandered a bit in North Dakota, but his great prowess as an athlete and as a great player on the invincible New York Yankees surely must be attributed to his days in the great North Star State of Minnesota."

BURDICK OF NORTH DAKOTA: "I say to my good friend from the State of Minnesota that we acknowledge that Roger was born in the State of Minnesota. . . . In his formative years, Roger lived in Grand Forks, North Dakota, and in Fargo, North Dakota. . . . So, in the years which really count he was in North Dakota."

HUMPHREY: "The real fact of the matter is that Roger Maris could never have been in North Dakota if he had not been born in Minnesota."

KEATING OF NEW YORK: "Before we forget, let us say a word for Mickey Mantle."

BUTLER OF MARYLAND: "I have listened to the discussion with a great deal of interest. It seems to me that Minnesota once had Roger Maris and North Dakota once had Roger Maris, but now New York very firmly has him."

KEATING: "The Senator is correct. We appreciate having him too."

HUMPHREY: "We are glad to do any little thing we can for the Senator."

KEATING: "It is not the first thing that my distinguished friend has done for New York. I want him to know that we are always friendly."

HUMPHREY: "We presented New York with Skowron . . . Blanchard . . . and Howard from Minnesota. I do not know how the New York Yankees would win without players from the State of Minnesota."

KEATING: "Or without the Twin Cities team. We are glad to have them in the league."

(A controversy over whether visitors in the galleries of Congress should be permitted to wear shorts, slacks, or jeans brought this story to mind for New York's Kenneth Keating:

"On a hot day in July, when tourists were lining up to enter the Senate gallery, an old gentleman whispered to the person behind him: 'Take a look at the little character in front of me with the poodle cut and the blue jeans. Is it a boy or a girl?'

" 'It's a girl!' came the angry answer. 'I ought to know. She's my daughter.'

" 'Forgive me, sir!' apologized the old fellow. 'I never dreamed you were her father.'

" 'I'm not,' said the slacks-clad parent. 'I'm her mother.' "

❨ While serving as Senator from New York, Ken Keating received an invitation to address a Memorial Day celebration. Enclosed was this unsettling program schedule: "This year's Memorial Day program will include a talk by the mayor, a recitation by a student, your speech, then the firing squad."

❨ As Senator from New York, in 1963 Kenneth Keating drew his colleagues' attention to one more subversive threat to the nation's well-being:

"Mr. President, it will come as a shock to many Senators, but according to a resolution of a certain Los Angeles civic organization the Communists have developed a new secret weapon to ensnare and capture youthful minds in America—folk music . . .

"The resolution adopted by this organization, called the Fire and Police Research Association of Los Angeles, Inc., describes folk music as—and I quote from the resolution —'an unidentified tool of Communist psychological and cybernetic warfare.' . . .

"Mr. President, this amazing document maintains that 'the dialectics of the Communist movement have successfully used, and are now using all modes and media of communication with young people, including the subtleties and the verbal subterfuges of applied dialectics in both poems and songs' and that 'it is becoming more and more evident that certain of the "Hootenannies" . . . in this country and in Europe have been used to brainwash and subvert'—and now, listen to this—'in a seemingly innocuous but actually covert and deceptive manner, vast segments of young people's groups.' It closes with a fervent plea for a congressional investigation of this 'unidentified tool of Communist psychological and cybernetic warfare' which is being used 'to ensnare and capture youthful minds in the United States as it has so successfully and effectively captivated them abroad.'

"I had always had the impression that if anything was thoroughly American in spirit, it was American folk music. To be sure, I was perfectly aware of certain un-American influences in it, like Elizabethan balladry, English Protestant hymns and spirituals, and, with respect to jazz and in some cases the Negro spiritual, native African rhythms. But in my naïveté I had never considered these un-American influences to be of a sinsister nature and simply passed them off as part and parcel of the melting-pot tradition which has contributed so much in the way of variety and interest to the American cultural heritage.

"In the light of this resolution, however, I have given this subject renewed attention. Have we ever considered, for example, that the music of our national anthem, 'The Star-Spangled Banner,' is based upon an English folk melody— a drinking song, no less—'To Anacreon in Heaven'?

"Of course, I realize that folk music tradition is grounded in movements of political, economic, and social unrest and I did not expect to find in music which originated among sharecroppers, miners, union organizers, factory workers, cowboys, hill folk, wanderers, and oppressed Negroes . . . a pattern of tribute and praise to such symbols of orthodoxy as the gold standard, the oil depletion allowance, and the standing rules of the U.S. Senate. . . .

"No one could possibly imagine the members of the

board of directors of General Motors sitting around a conference table composing ditties in honor of defense contracts, while it is not surprising that coal miners should
have come up with a protest song, 'Sixteen Tons,' crying,
'Saint Peter, don't call me,' cause I can't go; I owe my soul
to the company store.' . . .

"The first significant discovery I made was that from this
nation's very beginnings folk music had indeed been used,
'in a seemingly innocuous but actually covert and deceptive
manner,' to incite violations of the laws of the United
States. Why, even 'Yankee Doodle' has fallen victim to
misuse in this fashion, as it did during President Jefferson's
embargo of 1808 imposed to prevent our embroilment in
the Napoleonic wars. Just listen to this plea to run the
embargo:

> Attention pay, ye bonny lads,
>   And listen to my Fargo
> About a nation deucèd thing
>   Which people call Embargo.
>
> Yankee doodle, keep it up,
>   Yankee doodle, dandy,
> We'll soak our hide in home-made rum
>   If we can't get French brandy.
>
> I've got a vessel at the wharf
>   Well loaded with a cargo
> And want a few more hands to help
>   And clear the cursed Embargo.
>
> Yankee doodle, keep it up,
>   Yankee doodle, dandy,
> We'll soak our hide in home-made rum
>   If we can't get French brandy.

". . . Apparently, some of our folk music takes a pretty cavalier attitude toward the enforcement of our Internal Revenue laws and could easily brainwash our young people into total disrespect for all law and order. The song 'Darlin' Cory' is a prime example of this:

> Wake up, wake up, darlin' Cory
> What makes you sleep so sound?
> The revenue officers a-comin'
> Gonna tear your still house down

"Or, for another example, the now very popular, 'Copper Kettle,' which contains the lines:

> My daddy he made whisky
> My granddaddy did, too
> We ain't paid no whisky tax
> Since 1792.

"If enough people went around singing this at hootenannies, Americans might soon get the idea that they don't have to pay their taxes. After all, the family in the song got away without paying them for 171 years. And if the Government loses its ability to collect taxes to pay for our defense effort, we would be wide open for a Communist takeover, would we not?

"This sinister folk music plot for disarmament takes more direct form than merely inciting Americans not to pay their taxes. Consider, for example, this pacifist Negro spiritual:

> Gonna lay down my sword and shield
> Down by the river-side
> Down by the river-side
> Down by the river-side
> Gonna lay down my sword and shield
> Down by the river-side
> And study war no more.

". . . If we do not realize that this 'seemingly innocuous' Negro spiritual is 'actually covert and deceptive,' we have obviously been duped.

"Now the Communists have also been known to sow the seeds of dissension in capitalist countries by turning people against their own political leaders. There's an Ozark folk song—and perhaps one of the Senators from Arkansas can enlighten me as to its origin—that goes like this:

> Yes, the candidate's a dodger, yes, a well-known
> dodger
> Yes, the candidate's a dodger, and I'm a dodger,
> too
> He'll meet you and greet you and ask you for your
> vote
> But look out, boys, he's dodging for a note.

". . . These examples must give pause to every patriotic American who may have taken folk music for granted in the past. But there is one concern I still have about a congressional investigation of folk music such as proposed by the Fire and Police Research Association of Los Angeles. What I fear is that [it] would stimulate the writing of new folk music making fun of congressional investigations. This shows how devious the Communists really are. . . .

"Once a congressional investigation of folk music is held, the Communists set about composing new folk music impugning the integrity of congressional investigations, like this folk song of a few years ago:

> Who's gonna investigate the man who investi-
> gates me?
> I don't doubt my loyalty
> But how about what his may be?
> Who'll check the record of the man who checks
> the record of me?
> Seems to me there's gonna be an awfully long line.

> One more problem puzzles me,
> Pardon my strange whim,
> But who's gonna investigate the man who investi-
> gates the man who investigates him? . . .

"It all boils down to a gigantic plot; one that has been brought to our attention before, most notably, by the assistant minority leader, the senior Senator from California [Mr. Kuchel], based on letters he has received from constituents whose keen alertness to matters involving our national security is fully equal to that of the Fire and Police Research Association of Los Angeles, Inc. And so, now, to the list of subversive individuals, institutions, and ideas, which presently includes the United Nations, the income tax, the Chief Justice of the United States, the Girl Scouts of America, fluoridation of the water supply, the last four Presidents of the United States, beatniks, Harvard University, Civil Rights demonstrations, expenditures for mental health, the Arms Control and Disarmament Agency, coffee houses, every Secretary of State since William Jennings Bryan, professors of anthropology, back-door spending, metro government, Jews, *Time* magazine, the Council on Foreign Relations, firearms registration, the Protestant clergy, the two United States Senators from New York plus between 77 and 83 of their colleagues and proposals for Federal aid to mass transportation—to this list of Communist-inspired persons and ideas we must now add, merciful heavens, American folk music. And who knows what lies ahead?"

⟨ Kenneth Keating, former New York Senator, recalls that at times a man in politics, finding himself in a bipartisan atmosphere, may discover the sudden inspiration that saves the situation for him. As an example, he cites the story of a Mississippi law affecting squirrel hunting.

In this particular area it so happened that half the people were for the law, and half against it. During a certain election campaign down there, one candidate was making a rousing speech. After he had finished, he said, "Now does anybody have any questions?"

One man in the crowd said, "Yeah, how do you stand on the squirrel law?"

When the candidate's supporters heard that, they were scared, because they felt sure he'd say the wrong thing, but he said calmly, "Glad you asked me that question, sir. I understand that half my friends are for the squirrel law, and half are against it. I want it definitely understood that I stand with my friends."

❑ Former Senator from New York Kenneth Keating tells about the candidate for the House of Representatives who was orating with great verbal vigor before a street-corner gathering, during the critical preelection period.

One voter who had listened to every word shouted up to the candidate when he had finished his speech, "I wouldn't vote for you if you were Saint Peter himself!"

To which the candidate replied, "My friend, if I were Saint Peter, there's no possible way you could vote for me. You wouldn't be in my district!"

❑ In a 1959 speech before the Women's National Press Club, Senator Kenneth Keating of New York manifested a keen wit as he gave these incisive characterizations:

Lyndon Johnson: "He figures the best road to the White House is the Milky Way. He was the first man to try to turn outer space into a Congressional district. The other day he made his sixteenth denial of Presidential ambitions, a number roughly corresponding to the ballot on which he hopes to be nominated."

Jack Kennedy: "Jack has problems. Every time he appears on a TV panel show, thousands of viewers write in to ask which college won the debate."

Adlai Stevenson: "He still leads most of the Democratic polls. This shows Democrats have no desire to ruin the sport of the thing by any compulsive urge to win."

Hubert Humphrey: "Hubert is the first man to run for President on the basis of spending eight hours to answer a simple question. His talk with Khrushchev, I understand, is to be made into a movie called *The Lynx and the Larynx.*"

Democrats: "I've heard it said that there's only one real difference between the Democratic and Republican parties. The Democrat says things are awful and tells you a joke to cheer you up. A Republican says things are wonderful—and then weeps at the beauty of it. Actually I prefer another definition. We Republicans think of a person first as a taxpayer. The Democrats think of him first as a voter. Obviously the voters are increasing by leaps and bounds—while the taxpayers are a vanishing race. So how can you win?"

Walter Reuther: "He has announced that labor was not wedded to the Democratic Party. If that be true, we have been witnessing the world's most notorious case of living in sin."

⟨ Kenneth Keating defines the difference between an informed Administration source and a high Administration source as "five martinis at lunch."

⟨ Speaking at the 1959 Women's Press Club dinner, Senator Kenneth Keating stated that "Asking me to talk about the Democratic Party is somewhat like asking a man to manage his mother-in-law's campaign to be named 'woman of the year.' I suppose you expect me to say unkind things about the Democrats. . . . I have no such intention. Some of my best friends are Democrats. That is, Democrats for Rockefeller-Keating. Actually, the Democrats are not so much a party as a treaty of mutual nonaggression."

⟨ Republican Senator Keating made these remarks on the "carpetbagger" issue during his 1964 campaign against Democrat Robert F. Kennedy: "Why, there are people who have been standing in line at the World's Fair longer than he has been living in New York. . . . He thinks Tarrytown is a new brand of cigarette."

⟨ The Senatorial campaign in 1964 saw Robert Kennedy make proposals for large transportation and air-pollution projects involving the entire Eastern seaboard, provoking this comment from Kenneth Keating: "I can't figure out whether he thinks he's running for President of the United States or is looking for some kind of new federal job like High Commissioner of the Northeast."

⟨ During the 1964 Senatorial race in New York, Republican Senator Kenneth Keating avoided being pigeon-holed. "I don't like to be tagged conservative or liberal. I haven't made up my mind yet whether I'm a liberative or a conserveral."

⟨ It is generally agreed that one of the most serious problems confronting the world today is the population explosion. Cracked Kenneth Keating in 1965, "If it were not for the population explosion, there would not be so many versions of why LBJ accepted the 1960 Vice-Presidential nomination."

⟨ In March, 1963, Ken Keating neatly fielded a question of whether he planned to join the list of those planning to take a fifty-mile hike in pursuit of physical fitness: "A Senator mustn't be caught out in the country when the buzzer sounds for a vote. But I recommend the hikes for other federal types as the best way to reduce government *waist.*"

⟨ Noted New York's Senator Ken Keating in 1959, "During the campaign last year in New York, I was relieved of a lot of speech-writing of my own simply by quoting Jim Farley on the subject of Frank Hogan [Keating's opponent], Carmine DeSapio on the subject of Averell Harriman, Mrs. Roosevelt on the subject of Carmine DeSapio, and Arthur Schlesinger, Jr., on *all* subjects."

⟨ Barry Goldwater's plane circled over the Concord, New Hampshire airport in 1963, as on the ground Senator Norris Cotton gave the signal for the landing. Some minutes later the plane was still circling, and Cotton quipped to the control tower, "What the hell did you do—order him up or down? There aren't any votes up there."

⟨ In 1965 Republican Senator Norris Cotton was discussing the complexities of United States time zones and observed, "Many call standard time 'God's time.' It is not.

The rise of railroad transportation caused the setting up of 'standard time' zones.

"We had 'God's time' in the days of travel by horseback and stage coach, when time followed the sun changing a few seconds each mile. If we returned to it, Congress on Capitol Hill would be seven seconds ahead of Lyndon Johnson in the White House—and that would be something."

⟪ Senator Norris Cotton tells the story of a little old lady in the gallery who was bewildered by the loud ringing of the Senate quorum bells. Beckoning to a page, she asked, "Why are the bells ringing so frantically?"

The page replied: "I'm not sure. Maybe one of them has escaped."

⟪ In 1959 New Hampshire's Senator Cotton likened the legislature to a blacksmith's shop: "You have to spit on everything before you touch it; it may be hot."

⟪ Senator Norris Cotton of New Hampshire once made this revealing comparison of the two chambers of the Legislature: "The House maintains a barbershop, where Congressmen pay fifty cents for a haircut, but custom dictates that they tip an additional fifty cents, so it costs them a dollar. The Senate is different. You get the haircut free, but the traditional tip is a dollar. So, you see, the haircut is as free as most things furnished by the Government."

⟪ Noted Senator Norris Cotton about one particularly budget-conscious Congress: "The boys are in such a mood that if someone introduced the Ten Commandments, they'd cut them down to eight."

❨ New Hampshire's Senator Norris Cotton was flattered to receive a fan letter from a high school girl who was collecting pictures of Senators instead of Hollywood film stars. Her request for photographs, however, was accompanied by an ambiguous admonition.

"Please send me photos of twelve Senators," wrote the girl. "Please pick carefully; even the best are sort of funny-looking."

❨ When, in 1964, New Hampshire Republican Senator Norris Cotton announced his support of Barry Goldwater in his state's primary election, he was questioned as to whether this indicated a change in his hitherto "liberal" political views.

"Well," explained Cotton, "it's like the New Hampshire farmer. He was driving along in his car one day with his wife beside him when his wife said, 'Why don't we sit closer together? Before we were married, we always sat closer together.' The old farmer replied, 'I ain't moved.'

"I ain't moved," added Cotton. "I found the trend of Government has moved farther to the left."

❨ Senator Norris Cotton remembers the occasion years ago when, as a youthful orator for the New Hampshire Republican Party, he was called upon to address a certain town rally. Since the town was fairly distant, he took a friend along on the long drive to help pass the time.

As he delivered the speech, Cotton was quite impressed with his own eloquence, rising to new heights of rhetorical grandeur and power. Suddenly, however, he realized that he had been speaking for far too long and that his audience was approaching a semiconscious state.

He quickly apologized for his loquacity and announced that he would continue no longer. Hearing this, his driving companion, attempting to give him a little lift, yelled from the back of the crowd: "That's all right, Norris. Tell us all about it! We want to hear all about it!"

The meeting chairman, who was slightly deaf, glanced up quickly, then whispered to Cotton: "Don't pay any attention to that damn fool. He's drunk all the time."

([During the 1965 cutbacks on military spending that closed a number of domestic air bases, New Hampshire's Senator Norris Cotton quipped, "I am glad I am not an Air Force pilot. I could never take off on a mission without being in mortal terror that McNamara would close my base while I was still in the air."

([In February, 1966, Republican Senator Hugh Scott spoke before a Lincoln Day dinner in Medford, Oregon.

"Today is Saint Valentine's Day and I have brought with me some imaginary Valentine's gifts which I would like to distribute here tonight. You may recognize some of the names on the packages.

"For Vice-President Hubert Humphrey, I have here a stuffed doll of Bobby Kennedy and a package of pins.

"For the Honorable Robert Kennedy—Senator from New York, Massachusetts, and Virginia—I have Arthur Schlesinger, Jr., done up in pretty ribbons. They deserve one another.

"For the lovely Maurine Neuberger, I have a little note from Mark Hatfield. It says simply, 'Thanks!'

"Now, I have some gifts for the White House:

"Three Hot Lines, one to Ho Chi Minh, one to Mao Tse-tung, and one to Senator Fulbright.

"Also a box of pennies. The Great Society is the only place where they know how to flatten out a penny and sell it for a quarter.

"Also, something for Luci. It says, 'Herewith my permission to get married right after the press conference. Signed, Daddybird.'

"Also earflaps to protect the dogs at the White House.

"And a cushion for a soft landing on the moon.

"Now, for Averell Harriman, our roving Embarrasser, a notice that they are renaming the Ho Chi Minh Trail as 'Harriman's Highway.'

"I have here a two-week vacation at a Job Corps camp in Appalachia which I am going to send to Sargent Shriver, the Peace Corps dropout.

"A ticket on the French Line to inspect Dien Bien Phu goes to Lt. Gen. James M. Gavin, who believes our troops in Vietnam should hole up in 'enclaves.' "

❲ In August, 1959, Republican Senator Hugh Scott of Pennsylvania told an Almas Temple Shrine luncheon about the lighter side of Washington: "At the intersection of First and C Streets there is a structure that has a striking resemblance to a white elephant. Perhaps the less said about the New Senate Office Building, the better. Everybody has had a chance to express an opinion, most of it critical. But whatever may have gone wrong in the new building can be attributed to mechanical and construction failures, to the frustrations of engineers and committee members, attempting to adjust to the machine age, or perhaps, simply to the innate perversity of inanimate objects.

"Someday, after the earth has coursed around the sun a

few hundred times, and the moon, like any other delibera-
tive body has backed and filled from month to month, the
contractors will have emerged from their tunnels and sur-
rendered to the Senators their expanded underground
domain; clocks will move because there are able hands to
move them; mail chutes will operate according to the law
of gravity; the six bronze plaques in the cafeteria delineat-
ing for the ages the hot-dog-service line will give way to
other bronze memorials furnishing travel information to
the sandwich parade—all these things will order themselves
in time.

"Meanwhile, back at the ranch—the Old Senate Office
Building—our problems are more basic.

"In this building we are unhampered by luxury, new
carpets, doors for newly cut partitions in the walls or other
attributes of gracious living. We are at war with the world
of small animals.

"Along the basement corridors, even in the height of the
tourist season, mice outnumber constituents. The feminine
members of my staff report that mice are so numerous as to
cause considerable distress of mind. In fact, this may lead
to a female boycott of the basement floor except when absolutely necessary.

"Since the beauty parlor is absolutely necessary, even
though on the basement floor, attendance was unaffected
until one mouse ran into the shop the other day. This resulted in one lady's hairdo being completely altered from
its intended pageboy out to an unsupported stand-up
job.

"If the war of mice and women is not soon solved, the
mice and certain undelectable inhabitants of the world of
insectary may take over the whole building. This will force
a general hegira to the roach-and-rodent-free areas across
the street. If this happens, the wear and tear on the new
carpets will very shortly lead to demands for additional

appropriations. These will far exceed the cost of extermination of the unpleasant occupants.

"Perhaps this appeal should be directed to the Rules Committee. If so, come over into 'Mousedonia' and help us."

(Addressing the Pennsylvania Society of Newspaper Editors in 1959, Senator Hugh Scott spoke about the "Trials and Tribulations of a Vote Seeker."

"Last November 5 I counted my blessings in this order: First, I was a U.S. Senator, which had been my ambition for some forty-four years. Second, I was not going to have to run for reelection in two years, which had been my dream since 1940, when I was first elected to the U.S. House of Representatives—the chamber of temporary residents.

"Shortly after the election I went off to Hawaii for a vacation—the type that is often described as 'well deserved'! I don't know if I deserved it. But I can assure you that I needed it. I had campaigned (discreetly) in 1957 prior to the primary. I campaigned (hard) early in 1958 for the primary. And I campaigned (furiously) late in 1958 for the general election.

"For the first ten days in Hawaii the same nightmare woke me in the middle of each night. I dreamed that the election itself had been a dream and that I still had to campaign some more. It left me in a cold sweat.

"The chore of having to run for reelection every other year is so arduous that some members of Congress are relieved when they are defeated. A Representative who was defeated a few years ago was accosted by a woman on the street the day after the election.

" 'Mr. Cole,' she said, 'I know you. But I bet you don't know who I am.'

" 'No, I don't' said Albert Cole, smiling happily, 'and I don't give a darn.' "

⟨ Early in 1966 Pennsylvania's Republican Senator Hugh Scott had occasion to discuss "Public Relations Techniques —Potomac Style":

"Just last week we had a demonstration of a new White House technique for getting a critical chairman of the Senate Foreign Relations Committee off the front pages—call a 'summit' conference in Honolulu. . . .

"The White House has come up with an answer to London's colorful changing-of-the-guards ceremony at Buckingham Palace. The publicity reads: 'Visit the White House and see the changing of the pickets.'

"Even Washington's ministers have been unable to escape the artful techniques of White House public relations. Nothing gets a minister praying for the 'Great Society' faster than a sudden view of the President in the back pew. . . .

"The Vice-President had a long meeting with Ambassador Henry Cabot Lodge. Now they are saying: 'Cabot speaks only to Humphrey and Humphrey speaks only to Ky.'

"Another development in Saigon has been Ambassador Lodge's signing of a pact to introduce television to the South Vietnamese people. Some Americans who watch television in the daytime have charged that Lodge must be an agent for the Viet Cong.

"The President mounted a massive campaign for peace in Vietnam when he sent Humphrey, Rusk, Goldberg, and Harriman all over the world. The campaign had one success—*they* came back friends.

"Talking of Vietnam, the Washington press corps has reached the point where it yawns when Defense Secretary

McNamara makes one of his periodic announcements that we have stopped losing the war out there. They are waiting for him to say that the Viet Cong have stopped winning.

"The President, incidentally, has such a high regard for McNamara that he now says to critical newsmen: 'Let us sit down and compute together.' . . .

"The U.S. Travel Service at the Department of Commerce is planning to give wide publicity to reports that many Americans who are touring the United States, instead of going abroad, find the United States very much like Europe—full of Americans. . . .

"The space agency people, worried about Soviet competition, are working with the Travel Service on a campaign to publicize the fact that our 1.5-billion-dollar moon trip will be *American plan*—it will include meals. . . .

"And the information experts at the Department of Health, Education, and Welfare are worried about the recommendation that schoolchildren be taught how to drink alcoholic beverages. They have enough problems explaining dropouts to the public without having to worry about passouts."

❪ Dick Nixon analyzed his spiritual heritage in one of his 1960 campaign speeches: "My father was a Methodist, my mother was a Quaker. They got married and compromised and my father became a Quaker too."

❪ Republican Presidential candidate Nixon addressed these remarks to the citizens of Johnstown, Pennsylvania, during the 1960 Presidential race: "I really couldn't believe it when somebody said, when Mr. Kennedy was here, he referred to this place as Johnson City—you know, that's the only time he's mentioned his running mate's name since he has been nominated."

⟨ In 1965 Richard Nixon dubbed the first session of the Eighty-ninth Congress "the Xerox Congress."

⟨ Dick Nixon spun this story during his 1960 Presidential campaign: "When Yogi Berra went up to the World Series to play the first series with the Braves and the Yankees . . . one of the wives of the Braves wanted to meet the very colorful catcher of the Yankees. . . . Yogi was there, and she said he looked like a very cool fellow, and his answer was, 'You don't look so hot yourself.' "

⟨ During the 1960 campaign a reporter asked Republican candidate Richard Nixon about the kind of vacation he would take when the election was over, noting that he had never seen Nixon play golf. Responded Nixon, "Your comment . . . is probably the most objective comment about the quality of my golf that I've ever heard."

⟨ Just after President John F. Kennedy's inauguration in 1961, Presidential aide Ted Sorensen and Republican candidate Richard Nixon met, and the discussion eventually turned to Kennedy's inaugural address.

"I wish I had said some of those things," said Nixon.

"What part?" queried Sorensen, justifiably proud of his speechwriting. "That part about 'Ask not what your country can do for you . . . '?"

"No," commented Nixon. "The part that starts, 'I do solemnly swear.' "

⟨ In 1966 Dick Nixon kidded himself about being a "dropout from the Electoral College because I flunked debating."

⟨[Dick Nixon discussed "mudslinging" in a speech during the 1960 Presidential campaign: "I expect attacks in campaigns. One has been made upon me of which I have to take some recognition at this dinner. It was not made tonight but made previously. I hesitate to do it. It is of such a serious nature, however, that I think before this particular audience what I consider to be one of the worst smears in American political history has got to be nailed. I read it just a few days ago in the paper. . . . Dateline, Havana. Fidel Castro said, 'The two men running for President of the United States are a couple of beardless youths.'

"Now I resent that. I resent it because . . . after my first television debate, my makeup man said I had the worst beard since Sal Maglie."

⟨[Margaret Chase Smith, the Maine Republican, was once asked by a constituent, "What would you do if you woke up one morning and found yourself in the White House?"

Answered Mrs. Smith, "I would go to the President's wife and apologize, and then leave at once."

⟨[As the Administration's expenditures for the "Great Society" increase, Republican Congressmen seek clearer and more striking ways to impress their constituents with the real meaning of "A billion dollars."

In October, 1965, Minnesota's Representative Odin Langen tried this approach with a stag audience:

"If any of you men in the Seventh District had an extra million dollars in cash and told your wife to go out and spend it on clothes at the rate of $1,000 a day and not come back until she spent it all, you wouldn't see her for two years and nine months.

"But if you gave her a billion dollars and told her to go

out and spend it at the rate of $1,000 a day, you wouldn't
see her for 2,739 years!"

❲ Observed Indiana's Republican Representative Charles
Halleck during a 1961 "Ev and Charlie Show," "As far as
I'm concerned, I think we've been having too much government by leak. The only trouble is too many of these
leaks are real blowouts."

❲ Congressman Charles Halleck, ex-majority leader of the
House, notes that "the average Congressman . . . can
tell about all he knows in any given subject in five minutes.
Over in the Senate they have unlimited debate and it takes
them that long to prove that they know as much as we
do."

❲ Ex-Congresswoman Clare Boothe Luce tells the story
of a man who joined the circus and was assigned to clean
out the lion's cage. He was advised to look the lion squarely
in the eye and let him know he wasn't scared. After thinking this over, he turned the job down, saying, "I see what
you mean, but I don't think I could do anything as deceit-
ful as that."

❲ A legislator's reply: "Sir, my stenographer, being a lady,
cannot type what I think of you. I, being a gentleman,
cannot think it. You, being neither, will understand what I
mean."

❲ Like anyone else, Congressman William Widnall of New Jersey enjoys getting letters, but he was a little puzzled by the sudden arrival of sixteen separate copies of the same press release, all of which emanated from the new Department of Housing and Urban Development.

These were his thoughts on that February morning in 1966: "Am I that important or do they have a mailing machine that stutters? What if I only get one copy tomorrow? Have I fallen out of favor? Or is this just life in America's political capital? We dig our way out of one blizzard, only to be faced with another snow job."

❲ On the Senate floor in June, 1964, Republican George D. Aiken of Vermont borrowed the style of a currently popular satirical review to drive home a few barbs of his own:

"This is the week that is.

"This is the week that the hands of the clock are running in both directions.

"This is the week that King George III, lying restlessly in his grave for almost 200 years, has finally been vindicated.

"Poor misunderstood George—he always knew that colonialism was the ideal form of government. But the uncouth yokels—John Hancock, George Washington, Sammy Adams, and all the rest—they were too dumb to understand.

"They didn't know how well off they were, and they made trouble for George—real trouble.

"We must remember, however, that 'Might and right rule the world—might till right is ready,' and after 190 years during which George has been kicked and cussed and ridiculed by Whigs and Tories—Democrats and Republicans alike—'right' finally prevailed and the United States

Supreme Court decided, belatedly it is true, that George III
had been right all the time.

"It may be that some backward countries may now sneer
at us—but those that still hold colonies will applaud.

"And as for you, Nikita Khrushchev, you with your
crack-grained notion that legislative bodies should represent areas as well as population—please step down. Who
do you think you are anyway—Benjamin Franklin?

"This is the week that is.

"This is the week when Orville Freeman, bless his heart,
gave to the public the names and addresses of all the cotton
mills that copped 23 million dollars of taxpayers' money in
six weeks' time.

"What a shame—what a travesty to release these names.
Now, they will be the target of every organization that
believes itself deserving of a cut.

"Handouts are for farmers—and charities—and the
mentally retarded—not for high level manufacturers. How
could you do such a terrible thing, Orville?

"But now that the deed has been done and you boys in
the textile business are full-fledged members of the club—
we welcome you, Brother Bob, and you, Brother Charlie,
and all your comrades into the great fraternity of 'Feeders
at the Public Trough.'

"Let me caution you, however, that with the great privi-
leges which you will enjoy as members there is also an
obligation.

"Keep your dues paid up promptly. The voluntary contributions you made last winter were just initiation fees.

"The dues are regular and mandatory.

"This is the week when the 'Society for the Control of
Shyness' scored its greatest triumph.

"Willie the Wonder Boy had always wanted to be important but one thing had stood in his way. He was shy.

"He never liked to wrestle with the other boys. He would

never take candy away from the other children. He wanted it brought to him.

"Whenever he took a bath the water would be warmed for him as he had a violent aversion to cold water.

"Once, when it was suggested that he ought to act like other boys his age and get out and fight for what he wanted, he simply said, 'Nix on that stuff.'

"When his friends tried to get him to talk on television and radio, thinking that might cure his shyness, he was overcome by 'Ike-fright.'

"Then, the 'Committee for the Control of Shyness' took a hand with Willie. They appealed to his pride; they worked on his conscience and then they told him that the big bad escapees from rest homes and mental institutions would infest the country—and eat all the people unless he stopped being coy.

"That did it.

"Willie straightened up. He donned his gold-plated armor. He said, 'I want to do something big,' and promptly plunged into the swim, where he was almost, but not completely, immediately submerged by cold water.

"This is the week that is.

"This is the week that three red-blooded American boys are trying out a great experiment in psychology.

"These three boys—Lyn and Dean and Bob—had heard of a far-off country. At least, it seemed far-off until Bob found that it was actually within easy commuting distance.

"And in this far-off land there were lots and lots of people—so many, in fact, that it was very hard to count them.

"When Americans first visited this land the people were very glad to see them. They said, 'We like Americans—we want to work with them.'

"But after a few years this attitude seemed to change.

"In spite of all the presents the Americans gave them the

people of this far-off land became less sociable. They even got less friendly with their own government.

"One day they found that someone had broken into their palace and done away with their king—who really did like Americans.

"After that, they became less friendly than ever.

"One day not so many moons ago Dean said to Bob, 'I have just had a call from Cab. He says that most everyone in this far-off land don't like us any more. What can we do to make them like us whether they want to or not?'

"But Bob said, 'We must not do anything until we talk with Lyn.'

"So they talked with Lyn and he said, 'Do what you think best, boys, I will be too busy to help you much for four more long months.'

"So Dean and Bob, knowing that all backward people like candy, decided that the thing to do was to drop bom-boms all over these people who don't like Americans any more and that would make them like us immensely.

"So in this week that is we have been dropping bom-boms on the people of this far-off land so they will like us real well from now on.

"And if some of the bom-boms intended for the backward people along the Mekong inadvertently fell among the people along the Congo it may be that either Dean or Bob lost his sense of direction.

"Anyway, don't we want the 200 million people of Africa to like us too?

" 'Oil is oil' our boys are having a busy week.

"Yes, Mr. President, this is the week that is. A week to be long remembered.

"Provided, of course—and pardon this morbid note— that the events of this week do not constitute a prelude to the week that never will be."

⟪ Concerning the war in Vietnam, Senator George Aiken of Vermont noted in January, 1966, "I'm not very keen for doves or hawks. I think we need more owls."

⟪ Following is a sample of the humorous observations that come under the heading of "Overheard in the Cloakroom," a favorite feature of Colorado Senator Peter Dominick's monthly newsletter:

It is wasted effort to sit up and take notice if all you do afterward is stay seated. (2/66)

On inflation: It takes the average housewife about four checkbooks to fill one stamp book. (1/66)

Patronage personnel are like a broken gun—you can't make them work, and you can't fire them. (8/66)

If the going seems easy, you might just be going downhill. (7/65)

The Administration feels that living within its income is a fate worse than debt. (6/65)

They call it "take-home-pay" because there is no other place you can afford to go with it. (4/65)

There's a new drink out called Foreignade. It's the refreshment that never pauses. (2/65)

There's been so much publicity over the "Executive flu" going around Washington, Republicans are accused of attempting a croup d'etat. (1/65)

There are plenty of good five-cent cigars in this country. The trouble is they cost a quarter. What this country really needs is a good five-cent nickel. (12/64)

Did you ever figure to see the day in America when morality would be considered controversial? If this trend continues, we may soon be sending out Bibles in plain brown wrappers. (10/64)

Democratic Congressman Otto Passman of Louisiana when opposing the President's foreign aid requests: "I can give up postmasterships, airplane rides, and the sniffing of the roses." (7/64)

If we're going to ignore our military men, let's save some money while we're at it. Let's abolish West Point and Annapolis and the Air Force Academy. Then we can train our men at Ford and fight our wars in Edsels. (4/64)

The trouble with putting your two cents' worth in nowadays is that it takes five cents to mail it. (2/64)

I understand that the Supreme Court is going to extend its prayer decision and repeal bedtime. (1/64)

Every time another disaster strikes the Cuban economy, Castro makes a three-hour television speech. His new motto is "Better said than fed." (11/63)

On Fred Korth's real reason for resigning as Secretary of the Navy: "This is the first time the Navy ever used a supercarrier to lay a smokescreen." (10/63)

It looks like the only way we'll ever be able to balance the budget is to tax people what they think they're worth, not on what they actually earn. (8/63)

Isn't it wonderful! Secretary of Agriculture Freeman has gone behind the Iron Curtain to learn how they win every referendum. (6-7/63)

I hear they asked Lyndon to be a guest on *What's My Line?* and the panel couldn't guess. (5/63)

No need to worry about Ted Kennedy. He has no more influence in Washington than any other brother of the President. (4/63)

Castro Cocktail: Five parts vodka to one part Cuban rum. Mix in a red china bowl and top off with a nut. (4/63)

We may not be the first to reach the moon, but we'll probably be the first to send it foreign aid. (3/63)

Story going the rounds after Senator Kennedy destroyed a news camera during a recent skiing trip in New England: Jack to Teddy, "The phrase is 'managed,' not 'mangled' news, Teddy!" (1/63)

℆ Somewhat alarmed at the continued growth of the number of employees on the Department of Agriculture payroll in 1962, Michigan Republican Robert Griffin proposed an amendment to the farm bill so that "the total number of employees in the Department of Agriculture at no time exceeds the number of farmers in America."

℆ During 1964 the "carpetbagger" issue resulted in a Senate debate over the seating of the new California Senator, Pierre Salinger. A visitor approached one Republican Senator and said, "I hope you support the seating of Salinger. I'm from California."

The Senator replied: "It's too bad Mr. Salinger isn't!"

℆ Republican Senator Karl Mundt of South Dakota reports that the citizens of East Berlin, who have their eyes fixed upon the prosperous Western sector as a symbol of freedom, have managed to retain their optimism and a good sense of humor. He tells the story of a young East Berliner who had been told that his "mother" was the East German "Republic" and his "father" the Communist Party. Asked by Brezhnev what his ambition was for the future, he replied, "I would like to be an orphan."

❲ "Through my assignment to the Senate Appropriations subcommittee on interior matters," noted South Dakota's Karl Mundt in 1965, "I have had the opportunity to work with the Bureau of Sport Fisheries and Wildlife on a variety of items, including the effort being made to save from extinction the whooping crane. During 1965, while presenting a proposal for a research laboratory as a follow-up to studies underway to increase the whooping crane population, one of my colleagues whispered, 'Karl, the whooping crane population has increased to fifty—that's sixteen more than the number of Republican Senators we have. How about a program to save the endangered Republican species in the Senate!' "

❲ One day in mid-July, Congressman Alvin O'Konski of Wisconsin was making one of his rare speeches on the floor, and he concluded with these remarks: "This is the first time this year that I have taken time on any bill. And, before I close, so that I won't forget—I probably will not take the floor again—I want to wish you all a Merry Christmas and a Happy New Year!"

❲ The following is one of Arizona Senator Paul Fannin's favorite bits of apocrypha:

In a Texas courtroom, a witness was challenged by the opposing attorney on the ground that he didn't understand the obligation of an oath.

"Do you know what will happen," inquired the judge, "if you don't tell the truth?"

"If I tell one lie," replied the witness, "I'll go to the State Legislature. If I tell two, I'll go to Congress."

The judge held him qualified.

◀[Arizona Senator Paul J. Fannin reports, "I was told in 1964 that if I voted for Barry Goldwater that taxes would go up and there would be further war in Vietnam. They were right—I voted for Goldwater and taxes have gone up and there is more war in Vietnam."

◀[Illinois Representative Robert H. Michel, with some remarks from the Congressional Record: "The Labor Department is going to spend $141,854 of the Manpower Development and Training Administration's funds to train 700 jobless men in the art of diaper service. I realize that the poverty program must cover the waterfront. In this case it is pinning its hopes on a business that is in its infancy, but is generally picking up. There is constant danger of its folding at any time, of course. Some may claim that the Government is being rash by stepping into the diaper business. I tend to agree, and leave with you a thought borrowed from the slogan of the diaper industry—ladies and gentlemen, it's time for a change."

◀[It was 1959, and on the floor of the Senate the nation's image was at stake. A great debate was blooming, as Senators grew florid with the vehemence of their disputations. The issue: which flower to choose as the national emblem. The outcome: nothing, except to prove that reticence in the defense of the rose is no virtue, and garrulity in the pursuit of grass, no vice.

ALLOTT OF COLORADO: "Mr. President, in this hallowed chamber, we are approaching a somewhat weedy situation. Various proposals for designation of our national flower are springing forth like shoots after a wet spring. They threaten to overrun other even more vital issues.

"Therefore, I propose as our national flower, a true

flower, one which is the most widely grown cut flower in the United States, one which is perpetually flowering and knows no season, I present it in the spirit of Webster, Clay, and Calhoun, the spirit of amicable compromise. I offer for your consideration, Mr. President: the carnation."

KEATING OF NEW YORK: "Mr. President, I wish to express my personal gratitude to the distinguished Senator from Colorado for sending to me today a carnation to wear.

"However, I invite his attention to a fact with respect to which he may not be informed, regarding the proudest, oldest, and loveliest flower—the rose. I invite his attention to the fact that fossils of the genus *Rosa*, establishing the existence of the rose on this continent for more than thirty-three million years—considerably longer than this body has been in existence—were found in his own native state of Colorado. It is possible that this horticultural fact has escaped the attention of the Senator from Colorado, and that upon realization of that fact he may feel that Colorado should join the state of New York, which has made the rose its state flower. I sincerely hope that that will be the effect of my remarks today."

ALLOTT: "I agree that the rose is a very beautiful, fragile flower. It looks beautiful in a vase.

"However, I invite the attention of my distinguished colleague, who is one of my fine personal friends, to the fact that while the rose looks better upon the gown of a woman, the carnation is a flower which both men and women—and particularly men—may wear, with confidence in its ruggedness, its fertility, its virility, its courage, and all the other attributes that go with it."

KEATING: I think any flower looks better when worn by a woman than in any other surroundings.

"I appreciate the remarks of the Senator from Colorado, but it seems to me that he has added an argument for the adoption of the rose, because of all things we are seeking to accomplish in this world, one of the foremost is a closer relationship with our friends and allies. Perhaps the adoption of the rose as the national flower would tend to affect closer relationships."

DIRKSEN OF ILLINOIS: "Of course, English history records the War of the Roses, between the House of York and the House of Lancaster. I hope, after this long interlude, that the War of the Roses will not be resumed."

HICKENLOOPER OF IOWA: "Mr. President, I am distressed to hear what I consider to be the misguided arguments being advanced here today.

"The idea of a national flower or a national floral emblem is highly desirable, but I invite attention to the fact that some of us have introduced a bill proposing that the corn tassel be the national flower. The corn tassel is a very beautiful flower. It represents food, among other things. It represents the hope of our agricultural regions—and all states are agricultural. It represents the strength of our country.

"It seems to me that it is not only decorative, but it has great utility, which should appeal. While the rose is beautiful, and is grown in all states, and while the carnation is a wonderful flower, and has great sentimental value, being seen in profusion at funerals, and while I would not discredit the beauty of those flowers, I importune my colleagues to think about the stability and utility of corn, as represented by the corn tassel."

[RICHARD] NEUBERGER OF OREGON: "Mr. President, I should like to point out to my colleagues on the other side of the aisle that more roses grow in Oregon than in any other state, and that, unlike the corn tassel, the rose does not need price supports to enable it to flourish." (Laughter.)

MORTON OF KENTUCKY: "Mr. President, I wear a carnation. I might add it was given to me, free. I bear the carnation no malice. It is a beautiful flower. From the esthetic standpoint, it serves as a thing of beauty. I have not been able to find that it makes any great contribution to the welfare of our nation or that it is essential to our economic survival in this troubled world.

"May I point out that the corn tassel is not a full flower. It is merely the male flower. The ear of the corn is the female flower of the corn plant. I do not think we want to get into any controversy that is going to lose us the women's vote because of our adopting a male flower as the national floral emblem.

"I might add, incidentally, that corn is converted into various products. Some of this conversion takes place in my native state of Kentucky. I know from experience we do not want to get into a debate, on what should be the national flower, that is going to stir up the Anti-Saloon League.

"At the appropriate time I shall introduce the proper resolution. It is that grass be our national flower.

"There are those who say grass is not a flower, but I point out that grass does flower and seed. I point out that our first important resource is grass and that our most important resource is the cow. Let us look at the cow, the foster-mother of mankind. Where would the cow be, and, further, where would mankind be, but for grass? We are a meat-eating people. How could we satisfy our national hunger for meat, if it were not for grass, on which feed the animals that supply us with beef and mutton and lamb in such lavish quantities?

"It was grass that was mentioned first in the story of creation. It was grass, with its deep, penetrating roots, that gave fertility and protection to the great plains and prairie soils of America. It was grass that sustained the buffalo, whence came our forefather's food. It is grass that feeds the lowing cattle, the gentle sheep, the patient horse. It is to grass that we turn to heal our fields after they have been eroded and ravished by the plow and the cultivator. Grass is truly the hope of the conservationist and the dream of the naturalist."

DOUGLAS OF ILLINOIS: "Mr. President, I was somewhat surprised to come into the chamber and learn that the Senator from Kentucky was eulogizing grass as the national floral emblem. I think this is an attempted travesty on a very important subject. The Senator from Iowa has introduced a resolution making the golden corn tassel our national floral emblem.

"I think the Senator from Kentucky was attempting, in a very subtle fashion, to ridicule the resolution. Let me say this so far as the golden corn tassel is concerned. While I do not intend to reflect upon the chief product of Kentucky, which is grass, and very green grass—not blue, but green—I do want to say the golden corn tassel is the natural American floral emblem.

"What I am proposing is the golden corn tassel as a symbol both of the beauty and the bounty of the nation. Nothing could be more beautiful than a field of corn in full flower.

"Furthermore, corn is indigenous to the North American hemisphere. We have found minute ears of corn at least five thousand years old among the remains of the Indian tribes of the Southwest. I have in my office a photograph of a Mexican piece of sculpture of approximately 1100 A.D., in which the ears of corn are no longer minute but are almost as large as the normal ears of corn today.

It was corn which kept the Pilgrims alive during the first hard winter at Plymouth. It was corn which kept the Jamestown settlers alive during the first difficult winters. Corn went with the pioneers across this nation and furnished the main source of food for the settlers. Corn is now the chief farm crop of the United States. The center of the corn industry is of course in Iowa and in my own state of Illinois.

I will say to the Senator from Kentucky, a large part of the prosperity of Kentucky has been built upon corn, also—corn put into a liquid form. It is corn which perhaps should not have been imbibed by the people of this country, but nevertheless it is taken in a liquid form.

"It ill behooves the Senator from Kentucky to try to upgrade grass and downgrade corn."

MORTON: "I want to make clear I was not trying to ridicule the Senator's resolution. I know the Senator is serious and is perfectly sincere in his objective.

"I considered the case of corn, and I pointed out that the corn tassel is the male part of the flower and is not the full flower. The Senator will find Susan B. Anthony rolling over in her grave, should he make the fight for the corn tassel.

"With respect to the Senator's remarks regarding the contribution of corn in my own state, the Senator will find the Anti-Saloon League and the WCTU knocking on his door to say, 'Down with the corn tassel.'

"I merely bring out the point that the road before the Senator is a hard and rough road. I wish him well, but I intend to continue the fight for grass."

DOUGLAS: "I merely say we intend to keep up the struggle to have the golden corn tassel adopted as the American floral emblem."

4 . *The Democratic Wits*

❨ ON THE OTHER SIDE of the Congressional aisle sit—or just as often, stand—the Senators and Representatives of the Democratic Party. As we have previously implied, there is no such thing as *the* Democratic wit. However, despite allegations to the contrary by the Republicans, it is not true that there is no such thing as *a* Democratic wit. In fact, there are quite a number of them, as the following selections of legislative merriment are intended to demonstrate.

❨ Those who contend that the comic strips are a useless addition to our newspapers will find extremely interesting these comments by Senator J. William Fulbright in the Congressional Record of March 20, 1958:

"Mr. President, these are momentous times and the Senate is a very busy place. Yesterday was a particularly busy day for me and—according to newspaper accounts of domestic events—was a busy day for others as well. The

President met with a conference of State Governors to discuss ways and means of alleviating the distress of the current recession. The House of Representatives approved a Senate bill, an anti-recession measure, to increase the construction of new homes. The Senate, among many other activities, was the site of hearings to consider my bill to accelerate the construction of local public works already planned with Federal advance planning funds.

"In the midst of all these momentous events, Pogo, a comic strip opossum created by Mr. Walt Kelly and published in the Washington *Evening Star*, was expressing his frustration with the attitude and pronouncements of his companion character, one Albert the Alligator.

"I mention this comic strip situation because of certain events which have occurred in recent days. On Monday, March 17, I introduced a bill to aid the construction of planned local public works, and announced that hearings would be held on the bill on Wednesday, March 19. The executive branch of the Federal Government, meaning President Eisenhower's appointees, were immediately notified that the bill was introduced and that hearings had been scheduled for the 19th of March.

"Yesterday, March 19, these hearings began at 2 P.M. with the administration's witness in attendance. At approximately the same moment—2 P.M.—the bluestreak edition of the Washington *Daily News* was on the stands with a headline reading 'IKE MOVES TO SPEED UP JOBMAKING PROJECTS'—and the accompanying story relates a Presidential action to release $75 million of congressionally authorized funds to accelerate projects identical to those contemplated by my bill, S. 3497.

"One of the first statements made by the administration witness in commenting upon my bill—shortly after 2 P.M.—was that the bill was unnecessary because the President had directed him to ignore existing policy restrictions and to proceed at full steam to approve projects already contemplated by congressional authorization. To sum up the situation, I introduced a bill to accelerate economic recovery and the President immediately reacted by making available funds which he has had available since 1955—3 years before the current emergency became a political liability for the Eisenhower administration.

"Now I will get back to Pogo, the comic strip character. For those members of the Senate who may not be familiar with this very literate commentary on national affairs, I will relate certain matters in the background of last night's strip and quote certain portions from it. Pogo, the opossum, very much like the Senator from Texas in recent weeks, has attempted to suggest to Albert, the alligator, that certain courses of action are necessary and desirable. Every suggestion that Pogo has made has been accepted immediately by Albert as something already conceived and desirable beyond question.

"Last night's sequence contains the following exchange:

"Pogo: 'Doggone, Albert, I'm givin' out ideas an' you claims they's yours. Don't you think of nothin' alone ever?'

"Albert: 'I thinks of nothin' alone constantly, friend.'

"Mr. President, this exchange between Pogo and Albert seems to me to characterize perfectly the attitude of President Eisenhower toward the present recession and toward the Democratic leader of the Senate. Time and time again the President reiterates the view that there is no urgency— that things will get better in March—and at the same time he points with pride to his deep and fervent concern to combat a recession that does not really exist.

"Perhaps Albert paraphrases the true situation with Ike, when Albert says that 'I thinks of nothin' alone constantly.' Ike has never denied, in fact he apparently takes pride, that his team does most of the thinking for his administration. I have only one request to make of Ike—the team—and the whole Eisenhower administration: Please make up your minds. If you think the current recession requires action, say so unequivocally. If you think that no action is required, say so unequivocally. If you are uncertain, say so unequivocally."

❨ This excerpt from the Congressional Record of January 27, 1966, demonstrates Senator J. William Fulbright's aptitude for putting ironic indirection to its fullest use:

"Mr. President, from ancient times to the space age men of little vision have always preferred the petty pleasures of daily life to the glories of conquering new frontiers.

"In the ancient world a minority of cowardly Athenians resisted the great crusade against Syracuse but happily were overridden, with the result that—despite the loss of the entire Athenian Army and the subsequent fall of Athenian democracy—history has been enriched by a saga of valor and self-sacrifice justly celebrated by scholars from Thucydides to Walter Lippmann.

"History does not reveal its alternatives, but just suppose what might have happened if Leif Ericson had turned back from his odyssey across the fearsome North Atlantic and had left America to be discovered after all by Christopher Columbus.

"And what if Columbus had been thwarted from his great adventure by a niggardly and penny-pinching Queen? In all probability America would not have been discovered in 1492 as history so manifestly intended: indeed, it might not have been discovered until 1502 or even 1592. So what? you ask. So what, indeed.

"Or suppose the great Napoleon had been fainthearted and prudent and had stayed at home to fritter away the genius of the French nation on public works and public schools, on poetry and philosophy, and all the homebody tasks of converting the Revolution from dreams to reality. I can tell you what might have happened: the French might have gotten their liberty, equality, and fraternity but at the cruel cost of cheating millions of Europeans of the glorious deaths they died from Austerlitz to Waterloo. The costs to posterity stagger the imagination: Russia would have been denied an epic victory and Leo Tolstoy would not have been able to write *War and Peace;* America would not have fought its glorious War of 1812 and Francis Scott Key would not have been able to write 'The Star-Spangled Banner' with the probable result that we would all still be singing 'My Country 'Tis of Thee' to the hateful tune of 'God Save the King.'

"Today the pettifogging troglodytes have turned their small-minded malice against America's great adventure in space. In their ignorance and parsimony they tell us that there is really no hurry about going to the moon when tens of millions of Americans must spend their lives in dirty, dangerous, and unhealthy cities, when hundreds of millions of children around the world—some even in America—go to bed hungry every night, when hundreds of millions more are condemned to degraded lives of poverty and early deaths of preventable diseases.

"How tiresome these contentions are. How small minded and selfish and sentimental, how lacking in vision and idealism. To those Americans who grumble about voyages to the moon and the annual expenditure of $60 billion or more on weapons and rockets, I invoke the inspiring words of an ancient Egyptian slave who reproached a fellow slave for complaining about the chains and the beatings and the huge stones that had to be dragged across the desert to build the Pharaoh's pyramid. 'How tiresome you are to whine and complain,' said the one slave to the other. 'It is an honor to be associated with an enterprise of such magnitude.'

"Mr. President, a recent article in the great English journal, *Punch*, sternly but justly reproaches those Englishmen who would complain about giving up iron lungs and artificial limbs to provide the aluminum for rockets and space vehicles, 'as if,' as the article points out, 'a nation's prestige lay in its free artifiical legs, and not up there'—in the azure sky."

◖ It is always a source of considerable consternation for a public official to be introduced in laudatory terms that no one could live up to. At moments like these, Arkansas Senator J. William Fulbright frequently lightens things up with this tale: "A farmer was leading a cantankerous calf across a bridge. Halfway across, the calf froze and refused to budge. A car pulled up behind and the farmer, explaining the problem to the motorist, asked him to honk his horn. Maybe, he suggested, the noise might scare the calf into motion.

"The driver obliged. The horn roared and the calf, terrorized, leaped into the air, plunged over the bridge rail and drowned.

"The farmer, infuriated, turned on the motorist and upbraided him viciously for killing the calf.

" 'But you asked me to honk,' the driver protested.

" 'Sure,' said the farmer, 'but you didn't have to honk so big for such a little calf.' "

◖ Irony is always one of the politician's sharpest weapons, but it is difficult to sustain for as long as did Senator J. William Fulbright of Arkansas one day in 1963 on the Senate floor:

"It is a welcome relief, Mr. President, during these muggy, sticky, frustrating summer days, to be diverted even momentarily from the serious problems of government and public policy. We are indebted to the junior Senator from Arizona [Barry Goldwater] for providing us with such a diversion in his recent remarks to the Human Events Conference here in Washington.

"I read the Senator's speech with interest and enjoyment. It is indeed a remarkable speech. At no point does it burden the reader with the complexities of current foreign and domestic problems.

"The Senator has a rare gift of clarity. So lucid is his discourse that he makes us wonder what all the fuss has been over nuclear weapons and international tensions and unemployment and all the other stubborn problems that perplex the American people. In the Senator's penetrating analysis, all these problems can be made to evaporate if we will only declare a 'bold' and 'courageous' policy abroad and return to 'fundamentals' at home. It is regrettable that, for whatever excellent reasons, the Senator did not see fit to elaborate on his noble sentiments or to spell out how and where and by what means he proposes to take 'bold' action abroad or to explain to us which precise 'fundamentals' he would have us return to in our domestic life.

"Undoubtedly, the Senator from Arizona intends to do things in some future pronouncement. I think it only proper to assume that he will and, as a Democrat, I think I can assure the Senator that we on the majority side are prepared to wait patiently for the time when he will see fit to translate his brave theories into prescriptions for public policy. . . .

"We owe the Senator this forbearance because of his own gracious and generous attitude toward the Democratic Party. In his speech the Senator unequivocally expressed his opinion that Democrats are not Communists and that the Communist Party has not captured control of the Democratic Party—even though, in the view of the Senator from Arizona, the program of the Democratic Administration is viewed with favor by the Communists.

"I thank the Senator for his generous—I hesitate to say 'liberal'—view of the Democratic Party. In return, I am prepared to state my own unequivocal opinion that the Senator from Arizona is not a Communist either—despite the similarity of some of his views to those of the rulers of Communist China. I am sure this is purely coincidental.

"The Senator from Arizona is opposed to 'coexistence'; so are the Chinese Communists. The Senator is opposed to the nuclear test ban treaty; so are the Chinese Communists. The Senator thinks it is cowardly to try to avoid nuclear war; so do the Chinese Communists.

"I am confident that no fair-minded American will misinterpret the interesting parallel between the Senator's views on these matters and those of the Chinese Communists. The Senator, without doubt, is a loyal and patriotic American. . . .

"I was particularly interested in two themes that run through the Senator's remarks: his views on 'liberalism' and on 'coexistence.'

"The Senator is four-square in his opposition to 'liberalism,' which he regards as feeble and exhausted and at the same time—somehow—dangerously aggressive and predatory. 'Liberalism,' in the Senator's view, represents a whole category of evils that the Democratic Administrations of the last thirty years have invented to destroy the 'freedom' of the American people. 'Liberalism' stands for such wickedness as social security, which has destroyed the 'freedom' of the aged to be destitute or dependent; rural electrification and farm price supports, which have destroyed the 'freedom' of the farmer to live in poverty and deprivation by candlelight; public housing and urban renewal, which have destroyed the 'freedom' of many of our people to live in rural shacks and urban slums; public works and government fiscal policy, which have destroyed the 'freedom' of most—but not all—of our people to be blissfully unemployed; and federal aid to education—the most diabolical plot of all—which threatens to destroy our 'freedom' to be ignorant and unemployable.

"The Senator is opposed to all these incursions on the 'freedom' of the American people. He opposes them for many reasons, but most of all because they violate certain unspecified ethical 'fundamentals.' No doubt, in the fullness of time, the Senator will spell out these 'fundamentals.' . . .

"I, for one, am prepared to wait. It is rumored that the Senator from Arizona may be prevailed upon to seek higher office. Should that prove to be the case, he will undoubtedly spell out a dynamic program of national action under some stirring title like 'The Fundamentals of Illiberalism' or 'Let's Get the Government Out of the Business of Government.'

"As intriguing as the Senator's opinion of 'liberalism' are his views on 'coexistence.' 'To coexist,' according to Webster, is 'to exist together or at the same time.' The Senator, as we all know, is unalterably opposed to such an arrangement between the communist countries and the free world. It would seem to follow that the Senator considers it essential for one side or the other—presumably the communist side—to stop existing at once.

"The problem of course—which the Senator has not yet seen fit to comment on—is precisely how the Communists can be persuaded or coerced to terminate their existence. It seems reasonable to suppose that they will not do so voluntarily, so the problem is really one of compulsion. It is precisely at this interesting point that the Senator leaves us in suspense.

"He is absolutely clear, however, in his conviction that 'coexistence' is craven, cowardly, and un-American. It is, in fact, a communist idea, based on Khrushchev's apparent confidence that if the two sides engage in peaceful competition for the allegiance of mankind, his side will win. For an American to favor 'coexistence,' he would have to believe the democracy is far stronger than communism, that a free society can create a far better life for the individual than a totalitarian society, that freedom has a magnetism and promise for mankind that communism can never hope to match.

"Of this heresy no one can accuse the junior Senator from Arizona. He has stated unequivocally that he favors 'boldness and courage and determination' over craven 'coexistence.' These words, of course, are a bit vague and the Senator has not yet seen fit to translate them into specific proposals for a 'bold' and 'courageous' foreign policy.

"But perhaps we can speculate. Both the United States and the Soviet Union possess hydrogen bombs and intercontinental missiles with which to destroy each other's societies. Neither has the means of preventing the other from doing so. Under these circumstances the only alternative to 'coexistence' is mutual destruction. This, perhaps, is the key to the foreign policy favored by the Senator from Arizona —a 'bold,' 'courageous,' and 'determined' policy of 'coannihilation.'

"This, of course, is speculation because the Senator has not yet chosen to reveal his foreign policy proposals. It may be some time before he does so. In the meantime, there is nothing for us to do but restrain our eagerness and contemplate the delay with equanimity."

❨ Senator J. William Fulbright of Arkansas on sea gulls and society, 1963:

"Mr. President, I recently came across an article in *National Wildlife* magazine on the mores and mating habits of sea gulls. My initial reaction to the article was that I had learned somewhat more about sea gulls than I really cared to know, but on further reflection I realized that I was manifesting the rather stuffy and superior attitude which we humans all too often direct at our inarticulate fellow creatures.

"The sea gull in fact is a marvelous bird. Unlike many other species, it is entirely free of socialistic tendencies. It is in fact a capitalist bird, a rugged individualist with a highly developed regard for the sanctity of private property. Every family of sea gulls has its own nesting land, about seven feet square, and the family estate is absolutely inviolable. To invade one of these private preserves is the gravest of offenses, punishable by swift and stern retaliation.

"In addition to his sound economic doctrine, the sea gull is guided by rigorous standards of morality in his private life. Courting is conducted with dignity and ceremony and, once wed, the sea gull is monogamous and devoted to family. Divorce is unknown and scandals of the sort which rock great empires in the world of men are considered by sea gulls to be in unacceptably bad taste.

"More impressive still is the high regard which sea gull society holds for the principle of seniority. Every gullery has its venerated senior citizens, newcomers working their way up, and a few members whom everybody is allowed to pick on. Under the seniority system the young chick is required to keep his neck tucked in because a high head and a stretched neck is a status symbol among gulls. Nothing is more infuriating to an adult than the sight of a juvenile with his neck stuck out. This is the ultimate in presumption, and the bumptious youngster who holds his head high is likely to be struck dead by an adult who sees him. Where, Mr. President, outside a gullery and the United States Senate, is the principle of seniority more faithfully observed?

"The most ingenious and civilized of sea gull folkways are the rules of chivalrous combat. A head held high is the most heinous of offenses, but so long as a gull holds his neck in, he is immune from attack, even if he invades the private property of another bird. The tucked in head is a permanently available form of diplomatic immunity, sacred and inviolable. There is no real equivalent to it in human society except for certain rather limited forms of political asylum for heretics and dissenters. Surely with our superior mental endowment we humans ought to be able to devise a form of protection for our free thinkers and dissenters as safe and as convenient as the pulled-in neck.

"When sea gulls do actually fight, they seldom go beyond ceremonial expressions of hostility. When two enemies face each other, they are likely to stand puffing out their wings until one or the other commits the ultimate provocation of leaning over and pulling grass. So terrifying is this act that most fights usually end at this point. Only the gravest of conflicts actually reaches the point of whacking and biting.

"It takes little imagination to conceive of the benefits which would accrue to humanity if we were able to apply such civilized techniques to our own rivalries. Pulling grass hardly seems an appropriate expression of hostility for so elevated a creature as man, but certainly we should be able to devise more suitable forms of ceremonial combat. Consider, for example, the battle of Agincourt. It would have been almost as exciting and a great deal safer if the English had tipped their arrows with suction cups instead of sharp metal points.

"Or consider the hydrogen bomb. Wouldn't it be a fine thing if we could agree with the Russians to replace all our nuclear bombs with smoke bombs—huge smoke bombs which could set off immense unradioactive mushroom clouds and even make a tremendous noise but to do so without a lethal explosion. Surely it is not beyond the genius of modern science to invent such a weapon, one which would permit us the fun and excitement of nuclear war without getting killed.

"But all this, I suppose, is idle nonsense, suitable enough for the mindless sea gull but hardly worthy of the most exalted of God's creatures."

❨ Quips Democratic Senator William Fulbright of Arkansas, "It sometimes seems that a man can be arrested for unlawful assembly when he's just collecting his thoughts."

❨ During March, 1966, Senator Birch Bayh of Indiana was offering an amendment to the supplemental foreign-aid authorization bill. The amendment would require a "buy American" policy on purchases of iron and metal products for Vietnam. The Senator argued that United States aid funds were being used by Vietnam to purchase steel sheets manufactured in Japan.

Bayh argued that the Japanese product was not only overpriced, but also was inferior to the domestic product. "The Japanese steel sheets are twice as thin as those made in America," he claimed.

At this, Senator Bourke Hickenlooper rose and asked, "Twice as thin?"

"Half as thin," answered Bayh. Then, on second thought, he added, "No, make that read twice as thick." Realizing that he was in a bed of semantic quicksand, he smiled at Senator Hickenlooper and, turning to the official reporters, said, "Let the Record show what the Senator from Indiana *meant* to say, and not what he said."

❲ New Jersey's Democratic Senator Harrison Williams, Jr., who aligns himself with the liberal forces in his party, was listening patiently in 1959 to one of his colleagues' observations that a co-Senator was "a bit to the right of me."

"Oh," Williams shot back, "you've left him some room out there?"

❲ New York Representative Emanuel Celler, among others, objected strongly to President Johnson's 1966 proposal that the term for House members be raised to four years. Celler pointed out that two Representatives had become insane while in office, and, under the new amendment, would have been beyond the recall of the voters for two more years. Suggested South Carolina's Robert T. Ashmore, "Maybe they were driven insane worrying about the next election."

❲ During the 1964 campaign, a Democrat was imagining what would happen in the event of Russian missile attack if Barry Goldwater were President. "Informed of the attack, the heroic leader acts instantly to broadcast his instructions throughout the nation by television and radio. Clutching the microphone, he rouses his people to the defense: 'To your positions, men! Get those wagons in a circle.' "

❲ One Senator, a bit ruffled by the hard pace Lyndon Johnson was setting for the Legislature in 1959, complained, "Rome wasn't built in a day."

To which a colleague replied, "Yes, but Lyndon Johnson wasn't the architect on that job."

⟨[Stephen Young, Democratic Senator from Ohio, tells the story of a Congressman who pleaded with fellow committee members to vote out a particular bill with a recommendation for passage. A week later, however, he spoke out against the same bill, and voted against it.

Congratulating him, a colleague said, "I'm glad you've seen the light."

"Heck, I didn't see the light, I felt the heat," he replied.

⟨[In 1965 New York's Democratic Representative Otis Pike berated his colleagues in Congress for increasing almost all the President's national spending totals, and twitted Johnson's latest economy measure. "No wonder the President is serving coffee to members of Congress in paper cups at the White House," said he. "He'd be billions ahead if he could just turn the lights on and the Legislators off."

⟨[Senator Maurine Neuberger of Oregon related this story concerning a Southern Senator and a little boy in his hometown. Attending a recently integrated school, the youngster was walking home with one of his Negro schoolmates when the Senator asked him how he was enjoying school. "Just fine," answered the boy. "This is my friend Willie and he doesn't seem to mind that I am white."

⟨[Describing a puppy he had bought for his children in 1965, Texas Representative Eligio de la Garza noted, "It is a small per cent beagle—we don't have enough seniority for a 100 per cent beagle."

❲ In 1963 Ted Kennedy remarked to Georgia's Richard Russell that Russell, too, had been elected to the Senate while relatively young. "That's right, son," replied the Georgia Democrat. "But, of course, I'd been Governor first."

❲ When Senator Edward Kennedy was in the hospital after his plane crash in 1964, he was visited by his brother, Robert. A photographer lining them up for pictures said to Ted, "Move over, you're in your brother's shadow." He replied, "That's the way it will be when we are in the Senate."

❲ Ted Kennedy often tells this story in appearances in Massachusetts: "When I ran for the U.S. Senate in 1962, I worked day and night campaigning. I won by 285,000 votes. In 1964 when I was again running for the Senate, I was flat on my back in the hospital and couldn't do any campaigning. So my wife, Joan, campaigned for me. That election I won by over a million votes, the largest margin ever in Massachusetts. I still think some people believe they elected my wife to the Senate in 1964."

❲ "That '62 campaign was a rough one," remembers Ted Kennedy. "I shook hands with so many workers in so many factories in the western part of the state that at the end of one day I found myself greeting the men coming off the day shift in Schenectady, New York. But it turns out that my work wasn't wasted, because my brother Bobby carried Schenectady in 1964."

❲ Reports Massachusetts' Edward M. Kennedy: "I ran for the Senate at a very young age, and one of the issues used by the opposition was that I had never worked a day in my life. One day I was going through one of the factories in my state, to meet the workers. And I will never forget the fellow who came up to me, shook my hand, and said, 'Mr. Kennedy, I understand you never worked a day in your life. Let me tell you, you haven't missed a thing.' "

❲ During his 1962 campaign, Senator Ted Kennedy's wife and mother appeared on television in his behalf. Afterward, one irate man wrote and asked him, "What kind of a man are you that depends on women in your campaign?" The Senator replied, "What kind of a man would I be if I didn't depend on women?"

❲ Edward M. Kennedy often prefaced his 1962 Massachusetts Senate campaign speeches with this story about the two brothers who went fishing and one had a rod and reel and the other just had a pole, a line, a hook, and a can of worms, and that brother caught all the fish. So the next morning the first brother borrowed the pole, line, hook, and worms and went out alone and still didn't catch anything, but when he was going home, a fish jumped out of the water and said, "Where's your brother?"

❲ Reasons Ted Kennedy in defense of his extensive family, "If you're talking about too many Kennedys, you should have talked to my mother and father at the time they were getting started."

❨ In June, 1964, Ted Kennedy was injured in a plane crash. Recuperating in a hospital several days later, he was told by the doctor that he was doing quite well. Flat on his back but still in full possession of his wit, Teddy replied, "That reminds me of a story. A prizefighter was taking a pasting from his opponent. When he returned to his corner at the end of the round, his manager told him he was doing great, that his rival had scarcely laid a glove on him. So the fighter told his manager to watch the referee then— 'Because someone in there is beating the daylights out of me.'

"Doctor, I feel like that fighter."

❨ Encapacitated by an airplane accident in 1964, Ted Kennedy required two men to turn him over in his frame when it became necessary. Each time the process was ready to begin, Ted would say, "Okay, boys, the human rotisserie is ready."

❨ Eager to begin to walk again after his 1964 airplane crash, Ted Kennedy insistently pressed his doctors to set a date for him to take his first steps. Complained Ted, "It's harder to get a firm promise from you doctors than it is from a politician."

❨ Suggesting several possible Democratic candidates to run against Massachusetts' Republican Governor Volpe in 1965, Ted Kennedy named Mayor John Collins of Boston and Kenneth O'Donnell, former White House Appointments Secretary to President Kennedy. Commented Kennedy, "I do not know how it will come out but at least

Massachusetts is not like other states that are searching for candidates. We make up in fertility what we lack in discipline."

❡ Unavoidably detained by a late Senate vote, Edward M. Kennedy addressed the delegates at the Massachusetts Democratic Convention by telephone. Ted then concluded his conversation by ribbing his wife, already present at the convention. "I really am coming," he said. "Don't nominate Joan till I get there."

❡ Stated Ted Kennedy, before the 1963 Women's National Press Club Dinner, "I want to stay out of the limelight, out of the headlines—and out of the swimming pool."

❡ Addressing the January, 1963, dinner of the Women's National Press Club, Edward M. Kennedy insisted that "there is no reason to think that I am emphasizing the fact that the President is my brother just because I had a rocker installed in my Senate seat this afternoon."

❡ Discussing his brother Robert's climb of Mt. Kennedy in 1965, Edward Kennedy remarked that RFK "is not the first Kennedy to climb a mountain. I climbed the Matterhorn, which is higher, and I didn't need the Royal Canadian Mounted Police."

❡ Musing over his childhood, Edward M. Kennedy recalled, "While my father was certainly the fountain of all discipline, both he and my mother administered it. Justice was always immediate. No one ever said, 'Wait until your father gets home.' "

⟨["Money was hard to come by in my family," recalls Ted Kennedy, "and I remember allowances of ten and twenty-five cents a week. When I was in high school . . . my allowance was only a dollar and a half a week. . . . When it came to earning extra money, I sometimes cut the grass for neighbors. The pay was usually better than at my house."

⟨[Ted Kennedy was invited to attend a ski-jumping contest during the 1960 Wisconsin primary campaign. He accepted, with the reservation that, since he had never jumped, he would come strictly as a guest.

"I went to the top of the 180-foot ski jump and watched. . . . Then I heard the announcer say, 'And now at the top of the jump is Ted Kennedy, brother of Senator John F. Kennedy. Maybe if we give him a round of applause, he will make his first jump.'

"I wanted to get off the jump, take off my skis, or even go down the side. But if I did, I was afraid my brother would hear of it. And if he heard of it, I knew I would be back in Washington licking stamps and addressing envelopes for the rest of the campaign.

"I jumped."

⟨[Edward Kennedy reportedly leaped to his feet at a Temple Israel breakfast when the president of the brotherhood was introduced. Abashed, the Massachusetts Senator explained that he heard the phrase as "brother of the President."

⟪ During his trip to Ireland, Ted Kennedy said he was "glad to see a few cousins who didn't catch the boat," and announced, in departing, "we promise to come only once every ten years."

⟪ At the January, 1963, dinner of the Women's National Press Club, Senator Edward M. Kennedy reported, "I was down at the White House this afternoon with some suggestions for the State of the Union address, but all I got from *him* was, 'Are you still using that greasy kid stuff on your hair?'"

⟪ During his Massachusetts Senatorial campaign in 1962, Edward Kennedy told the story of "these three boys who rescued Jack while he was out swimming." The President gave each boy a wish. The first wanted an appointment to West Point, and the second wanted an appointment to Annapolis. The third wanted to be buried at Arlington Cemetery, because when he told his father who he had saved, he would be shot. "But," remarked Ted, "I know that doesn't apply to any of you wonderful fathers sitting here tonight."

⟪ Kentucky Representative Charles Farnsley is one of the nation's notable college dropouts. "I was studying Municipal Government at the University of Kentucky," reports Farnsley, "when I was elected mayor of Louisville."

⟪ Sidney R. Yates, Democratic Representative from Illinois, believes that despite the United Nations' shortcomings, there is no practical alternative to the situation. The organization's difficulties put Yates in mind of the mouse that was employed by the Space Administration and was grumbling to his friend: "They stuff me into a nose cone until I can hardly breathe," he said. "Then they shoot me a mile high into space through magnetic belts that shock me; then they dump me into the sea and almost drown me. Then they put me on the laboratory table and stick pins into me."

The mouse's friend sympathized. "That's awful! Why don't you go back to your old job?"

"What!" cried the mouse. "Back to cancer research?"

(Having seemingly reached an impasse in the debate on a 1959 tax bill, Illinois Senator Paul Douglas compared the bill to the Latin verb *"aio."* Analogized Douglas, "It is present, it is imperfect, it is impossible to decline, and it has no future."

(One of the most important projects to Senator Paul Douglas of Illinois is the founding of the Indian Dunes National Lakeshore on Lake Michigan. Noted the Senator in 1965, "Until I was thirty, I wanted to save the world. Between the ages of thirty and sixty, I wanted to save the country. But since I was sixty, I've wanted to save the dunes."

(Illinois Democratic Senator Paul Douglas, in introducing his "truth-in-lending" bill for the fourth time at the Eighty-ninth Congress' first session in 1965, treated his colleagues to this short history of interest rates:

"A study of the history of interest rates will reveal that truth in lending legislation is nothing new. For example, over 37 centuries ago in 1800 B.C. the king of ancient Babylonia decreed that all loans had to be accompanied by a written contract setting forth the terms of the loan. Moreover, if through subterfuge, a higher than legal rate of interest was actually collected, the principal of the loan was forfeited to the borrower.

"Mr. President, at the risk of sounding like the archest of reactionaries, I merely want to observe that if the prevention of subterfuge on interest rates was good enough for ancient Babylonia, it is good enough for us.

"It should also be pointed out that interest gouging has enjoyed an equally long, if not honorable tradition. In ancient Greece, loan sharks in Athens were known to have charged interest at the rate of 48 percent a month, or 576 percent a year. And in the 15th century, Italian bankers charged the King of France 100 percent interest on a war loan while local merchants were borrowing at only 5 percent. Apparently, the King of France was not considered to be a good credit risk.

"During most of the Middle Ages, however, the 'just price' doctrine was followed in regard to the loaning of money. An interest rate of more than 6 percent was regarded as usury and this judgment was backed up by the medieval church, which felt that ordinary citizens were at a disadvantage in dealing with sophisticated and worldly money lenders. The church, therefore, established and enforced the 6-percent 'just price' doctrine to protect the public interest.

"The historical and moral sanctity given to the magic figure of 6 percent survives to this very day and many lenders go to great pains to disguise the fact that they are charging more than 6 percent per year. Of course, the buy now pay later installment plan was unheard of in the Middle Ages, and it would be unrealistic to expect anyone to profitably loan money at 6 percent in many areas of today's consumer credit market. Nevertheless, the reverent attitude accorded the historic 6 percent still survives."

❰ Democratic Senator Paul Douglas offered this explanation of Stuart Symington's prestige among his colleagues in 1959: "He drinks with the South and votes with the North."

❰ Toward the end of the Congressional session in 1962— an election year—a newsman suggested to Montana's Senate majority floor leader Mike Mansfield that many Legislators were praying for adjournment. Replied Mansfield, "If I pray any more, I'm going to have housemaids' knee."

❰ Representative Morris Udall of Arizona, when discussing his state's long quest for additional water, recalls the maiden speech of Senator Henry Fountain Ashurst.

"Mr. President," began the Arizona legislator, "the baby state I represent has the greatest potential. This state could become a paradise. We need only two things: water and lots of good people."

He was interrupted at this point by a hardened senior Senator from New England, who pointed out, "If the Senator will pardon me for saying so, that's all they need in Hell."

❰ Arizona Congressman Morris Udall, like most of his colleagues, attends numerous "coffees," and often thinks "on those occasions of Winston Churchill, who once was seated at a formal dinner next to a very opinionated, vociferous lady who berated him throughout the evening on his policies, program, and activities as Prime Minister. Finally, she said with complete exasperation, 'Mr. Prime Minister, if I were your wife, I would put poison in your coffee.'

"Sir Winston replied, 'Madame, if I were your husband, I'd drink it.' "

❨ In debating budget appropriations, Congressmen notoriously guard their own projects dearly, but slice willingly away at the recommendations of their colleagues. This state of affairs reminds Arizona Congressman Morris Udall of this story: "Hanging his coat on a restaurant rack, a man sat down to dine. A thief seized his coat, put it on, and began to run away. The coat's owner, enlisting a nearby policeman, gave chase. The officer ordered the thief to halt; when he kept on running the coat-owner shouted, 'Shoot him in the pants!' "

❨ New Jersey Representative Charles Joelson was happy to report to his constituents in 1965 that the Treasury's award of a 3-million dollar contract for the manufacture of dimes and quarters had gone to the Dupont Company. Remarked the Congressman, "I am glad that some employees of my Congressional district will . . . be making money."

❨ Upon moving from New York City to Baltimore in 1964, poet Ogden Nash received a warm welcome from the Republican mayor of that city. The occasion inspired Maryland's Democratic Representative Carlton Sickles to write:

"Dear Mr. Poet
I want you to know it
Is widely considered a coup
When from the bustle
We're able to hustle
An asset as peachy as you.

P.S.

Although in your field I
Scarce rank as an artisan
I did want it clear that
Your welcome's bipartisan."

❲ Newspapers in 1959 headlined the controversy of Congressional nepotism, giving as an example one Representative whose son was being paid almost $12,000 for aiding his father. Another Congressman remarked, "I'd do the same, but I'm afraid my replacement in 1960 wouldn't keep the boy on."

❲ Missouri Senator Stuart Symington remembers his first date with Miss Evelyn Wadsworth, who was to become his wife, and whose father was himself a Senator: "I rang the bell. The butler answered it. I'd never seen a Senator and I'd never seen a butler in a dress suit. So when a great big impressive-looking man came to the door, I stuck out my hand and said 'How do you do, Senator?'

"It must have set me back with her folks for a year."

❲ Senator Stuart Symington of Missouri addressed the 1960 Presidential Campaign Kick-Off Dinner in Washington in January, 1960: "Mr. President, Mr. Chairman, Mr.

Speaker, distinguished guests, my fellow Democrats—and all Rockefeller fans who saw our light in the window. I thank you, most sincerely, for including me in your 'Parade of Prospects.' I do appreciate the honor, and believe I know what is expected on this occasion tonight.

"The prospect should demonstrate: The *brain* of a Thomas Jefferson. The *common sense* of an Andrew Jackson. The *humanity* of a Franklin Roosevelt. The *courage* of a Harry Truman. . . . In seven minutes!

"And somewhere in the course of his remarks, he really should spell out a bold new foreign policy, a method for balancing the budget, and an adequate farm program.

"It is not exactly the easiest assignment in the world. But—you notice nobody backed off from it. Everybody wants to run for President this year. And I know why. 1960 is another 1948, if there ever was one. Note the similarity: The pulse-feelers and trend-watchers say we don't stand a chance. The poll-takers are committing us to the undertakers. And I'm sure that certain newspapers already have our funeral notice set up in type.

"But don't you believe it. In the words of that great Missourian Mark Twain: 'The rumors of our death are grossly exaggerated.' "

(Senator Abraham Ribicoff of Connecticut opened his remarks before the 1965 National Convention of Citizens for Educational Freedom with an anecdote about a friend who had gone into a toy store to purchase a gift for his son. "After a quarter of an hour's browsing his eye lit on a fascinating gadget—colorful plastic circles and loops that were marvelously intertwined. He played with it for a bit, then timidly approached a saleslady.

" 'Pardon me, Ma'am,' he said, 'could you tell me what this is?'

" 'That, sir,' she answered, 'is an educational toy.'

" 'Yes,' he persevered, 'but I don't understand it. I can take the pieces apart, but I can't fit them together again.'

"The saleslady smiled benignly. 'Exactly,' she said. 'No matter how you fit it together it never comes out right. It's to teach the child to adjust to the modern world.' "

❨ In April, 1965, Senator Abraham Ribicoff addressed the League of Women Voters in New London, Connecticut, and began, "About four weeks ago the syndicated cartoonist Jules Feiffer published a cartoon as remarkable for its insight into contemporary attitudes toward poverty in the United States as it was for its bitterly instructive irony.

"Feiffer represents a tired, thoroughly 'beat' old man in tragi-comic soliloquy. Feiffer has his old man saying to himself, 'I used to think I was poor. Then they told me I wasn't poor, I was needy. They told me it was self-defeating to think of myself as needy, I was deprived. Then they told me underprivileged was overused. I was disadvantaged. I still don't have a dime. But I have a great vocabulary.' "

❨ In 1965 Minnesota's Democratic Senator Eugene McCarthy was convinced that the United States was overreacting to the problems of the gold drain and the balance of payments. When Henry H. Fowler, the President's nominee for Secretary of the Treasury, was before the Senate Finance Committee, McCarthy asked him if he thought the problem mainly economic or psychological. Fowler admitted he believed the problem psychological, whereupon McCarthy replied, "Then why not put trading stamps into the National reserve?"

❴ Here is the text of a speech by Senator Eugene J. Mc-
Carthy of Minnesota, before the Gridiron Club dinner in
March, 1961:

"Just before I arose to speak, the Secretary of the Interior, Mr. Udall, asked me, 'Why did they pick you?' I had
given some thought to this question myself and concluded
that I might have been asked for several reasons. I've been
designated as spokesman for the liberals; this is a designation one can get without really seeking it. The liberals
really haven't fully accepted this administration yet. The
liberals are hard to please. They like to think of themselves
as something like the Hungarian Government in exile—
they're uneasy when they're in the majority. I have thought
once or twice about resigning from the ADA, but it sounds
so bad to say that I was a former member. My defense,
when hard pressed, is to say I'm a member for the FBI.

"There may be a better reason for my having been
chosen, however. The President and I have much in common. Both of us nominated Adlai Stevenson for President.
He in '56, and I in '60. There was some difference in our
timing. As a matter of fact we had a lot in common even at
the 1960 convention: we had the same set of candidates for
both offices. We just didn't sort them out quite the same
way. I had only one candidate for Vice-President. I had
almost every other for the Presidency. He had many candidates for the Vice-Presidency along the way—and at the
convention.

"When I ran for the Senate in 1958, there were some
newspapermen who said that my race was a test for candidate Kennedy. In Minnesota I, as a Catholic, won over a
Lutheran, and I might add, I had trouble with the clergy
—before the election—and that is when it's real trouble. I
was younger than my opponent. I was said to be less experienced. I was called an intellectual—I've found that a little
learning goes a long way in politics. But, in any case, when

all was over, a number of astute newspapermen wrote articles saying that I had proved that one with all these handicaps could win. I was quite set up until I overheard some say that my election might have proved all these things, but on the other hand it might have proved that anybody could win. Once one is elected, he shouldn't look too closely at the votes or seek reasons as to why people did vote for him.

"There is a third possible reason to even up things. I'm sure that candidate Kennedy had a hard time deciding between Governor Freeman and me when he looked about for a nominator, because—well, both of us have had experience. We had both nominated Hubert Humphrey. This is a severe test.

"I want to say a word for the press before I go on to talk about Democrats and Republicans. I don't want to say that I have sympathy for members of the press; I have admiration for them. The press has never bothered me very much either for good or bad. This is a problem for House members—and young Senators, I might note. In the course of the Eisenhower Administration I thought that Washington press corps members really proved themselves, not only as political reporters but as religious and medical reporters as well. In the Administration of Harry Truman, the reporting—political reporting that is—was relatively simple. President Truman was a Democrat and took a pretty clear stand. If a reporter had to get into religion, it was relatively simple. Once in a while some Baptist would want to throw Truman out, but he'd refuse to go. A reporter might have to write about a swear word once in a while, or that the President played poker and took a drink, but the religious reporting was quite simple in that administration. And the medical reporting was quite simple too—an occasional case of indigestion—but that was about the extent of it.

"With the Eisenhower Administration things became very complicated. In the campaign, the candidate and most of his supporters said that their approach to politics would be different. They said that it would be nonpolitical; that it would be moral and spiritual. This should have served as a warning. After the election, the problems became acute. It was hard to sort out the politics from the religion. It was even harder to sort out the religion.

"I think that Bill Miller, who wrote a little piece called 'Piety Along the Potomac' in those days, had it about right. This was not written about the President's personal piety, but rather about the generally pious air that prevailed throughout the Administration. He described it as a very vague religion very strongly held to—somewhat like their politics. Well, you can't say the same about the religion of this Administration. It is complicated, dogmatic, and even involves canon law. This has put a new burden on the press. I might note that for centuries one great religious controversy was over private interpretation of the Bible, but now it's moved over to private interpretation of the Constitution. This opens up a whole new field, and I think I ought to warn the members of the Supreme Court who are here that they had better begin to guard their field. If private interpretation goes too far, the judicial hierarchy may be threatened.

"It is in the field of medicine, I think, that the new challenge to the press really exists. The press by the end of the Eisenhower Administration had a pretty good knowledge of all the illnesses of the male who had passed his peak—geriatrics, in general. And then along came a new campaign and a new Administration, and the press has had to move on now to—well, obstetrics to begin with. This is just the beginning. Now we're in pediatrics, and this can go on, I say, almost without limit.

"Most Democrats for a number of reasons were reluctant to see the Eisenhower Administration go. Politicians like to have a target. The Eisenhower Administration was a target—a moving target—just barely. Democrats, too, are generally rather sporting fellows. When we get near a sickbed or around an undertaking establishment, we become very kind and gentle. I don't mean to say that the Republicans have quite reached this state. They do have the gift of survival. At their high points of life, Republicans are not very vigorous, but, on the other hand, in the period of decline they are like the lower forms of plant and animal life: it's really hard to destroy them. They have a potential for survival. Today they're somewhat dormant or hibernating, but there is life in them. I want to assure all Democrats that we must remain on guard.

"Democrats hated to see the Eisenhower Administration go for another reason. It's like missing the last section of a serial which began back in 1953, soon after the successful election, when the Republican chairman, Leonard Hall, announced—in quite a formal way—that Republicans were going to remake the Republican Party in the image of President Eisenhower. It seemed like an interesting undertaking—a kind of reincarnation. This effort went on for a while and nothing seemed to happen, and then the word came out that a man named Arthur Larson had written a book called *A Republican Looks at His Party*. And the next word was that the President had read it. This was later denied. I think it was Ed Folliard who scooped everybody. In any case this book was accepted as the word on Republicans. In it they found that they already were what they thought they had to make themselves. This simplified their problem a great deal. This period—1956–57—was the high point for Republicans. They developed wonderful phrases: 'progressive moderation,' they said characterized the party—a gradual slowdown. We didn't know what it meant, but this was what was going on. Then they got really enthusiastic, and they said they were 'standing,' as I recall it, 'firmly astride the authentic American center, grasping the American consensus.' A frightening image, if you look at it too closely.

"Republicans were shocked in '58 in the Congressional elections and decided that they needed another reexamination. The Administration set up a special commission to determine goals for America. Some of us thought it was a little late in the Administration to set up that commission. The Republican Party set up at about the same time a committee to determine what the Republican Party stood for. That committee reported shortly before election, and the chairman, Mr. Percy, said that he could summarize what the party stood for in these two words: 'dynamic conservatism.' And that's where they left it as they went into the campaign.

"There were really three kinds or three levels of Republicanism in the campaign. There was the most advanced group, who said there are problems and something should be done about them—but not at this time. There was another group made up of those who said that there are problems—they were considered a little bit forward-looking. There was a third group that said there are problems and we ought to do less about them than we're doing now. And then Rockefeller came along and he spoiled everything. He said there are problems, and we ought to do something about them—*now*. When he said 'now,' things began to come apart. The Republican candidate was doing very well up to this point. He had one foot in each of three camps, but to put one in the fourth—this was too much for him. He was like the proverbial chameleon who got along well until he tried to cross a Scotch plaid, and at that point, as the poet said, true to his chameleon instincts, he died.

"Success for the Democrats with their candidate and with their program was almost inevitable. Now we have a new Administration. I believe there is a significant point of contrast between the last Administration and what we've seen of this one—and it may be a little bit early to pass any very final judgment on it. But I would go so far as to say this: that—well—it's the line that the music critic used in talking about Liberace. The critic said that he didn't know whether Liberace played well, but that he surely played fast.

"But the great point of contrast is, I think, in the manner in which people have accepted appointments in this Administration—in contrast with the manner in which they accepted appointments in the last. The men called to the New Frontier—well—it's almost like something out of Exodus: you get the impression that they're standing with their shoes tied and their loins girt, staff in hand, and when the call comes, why—they leave!

"In the last Administration, you may recall, there was hesitation; there were apologies; there was reluctance. Why, I remember when Ezra Benson was asked to come. He was reported to be in a state of indecision for about two weeks. He finally—well, he made this statement in Utah—he said he received a witness from the Almighty that he was to go—and with that recommendation he came. But in the case of Governor Freeman, why, he was almost like Cincinnatus. He just dropped the plow right in the furrow. Of course they say—the real classical scholars say—that Cincinnatus was never found plowing any place except on the front forty where the messenger came.

"When Mr. McKay came in as the Secretary of the Interior, he left his Chevrolet dealership with reluctance. Secretary Udall just beached his canoe, dropped his paddle, and on he came.

"Perhaps the most striking contrast relates to the office of Secretary of Defense. And here we had a fair basis for comparison because both men were called from the automobile industry. Mr. Wilson of General Motors came reluctantly. You may remember how he reconciled his devotion to General Motors and to the country. Mr. McNamara didn't say anything of the kind. Both were ground transportation men, and both had some similar troubles. Mr. Wilson didn't know that space existed or was indifferent to it, and Mr. McNamara had trouble too until some of those philosophers from Harvard took him aside and gave him a lesson in relativity. After he got the word on relativity, why, he understood something more of politics and missile gaps and some of the other problems of space. In any case, Mr. McNamara came quite eagerly. He came without any particular apologies to Ford or any protestations as to what he was giving up. I might note for Mr. McNamara if he still communicates with Ford and if there's no conflict of interest (I hope that the President will excuse him in this instance if there is because this is an old issue)—there's the problem of the Edsel. Senator Goldwater has been talking about the forgotten man. The forgotten man is defined as the fellow who is on the way up but isn't sure he's going to make it, or the man who's on the way down but doesn't want people to know it, or the one who has kind of given up. And it seems to me that this is just about what Ford Motor had in mind for the Edsel. The Edsel could become the Volkswagen for the forgotten man in the Goldwater Administration. I do hope that if you've got those old plans lying around, Mr. McNamara, you will tell Ford to hold on to them at least until after 1968.

"There is another difference, not only in the manner of coming but in the nature of the call. Today President Kennedy calls. In the Eisenhower Administration there was simply 'the call.' Nobody knew who called, but the call came. The only man who wasn't called was George Humphrey. One got the impression that the President, after being inaugurated, went out on the White House lawn and there was George under the oak tree, and that George, when asked how he got there, said, 'Before you were, I am.'

"Well, from that time on everybody was being called in and called back. Roger Keyes was called in, then called back. Mr. Anderson was called in for one purpose, and then we were told called back, and then he was recalled as Secretary of the Treasury. Neil McElroy received a kind of call. I think his song was 'I Hear My Pension Calling' when he finally departed. This was more or less the way it went. And then came the departures, for the most part quiet and willing. There were one or two who went with joy. Jim Mitchell was one of these. You know, the word we had was that during the last year or two of his service, before going to work he used to have his wife pull the rug out from under him two or three times. He'd take two falls forward and two back, and then he was ready to go to the White House.

"There is one exception, however, I understand, and that was the case of Mr. Summerfield. He came reluctantly and threatened to quit once or twice. This was before he discovered the wonderful world of books. And after that, they say, he was hesitant about leaving. He was undecided. There were two ways open to him: one to be a librarian, and the other to be a gamekeeper. He hasn't quite decided as to which of these vocations or occupations he ought to follow. . . ."

❨ As chairman of the Appropriations Subcommittee, in September, 1965, Representative Otto Passman of Louisiana was lamenting the restraints that had been placed upon his handling of the current aid bill. He likened himself to a rooster whose wings had been clipped, but promised not to try to "fly over the fence" by voting against the bill.

"I will listen to my own flock cackle—and I will do a bit of crowing—but I am not going to try to fly out of the yard." But, he added pensively, "I do hope my wings will sprout again."

⟨ Representative Emanuel Celler of New York has a few retorts he likes to use when people give him particular difficulty. For instance, to an opponent who has said nasty things about him, Celler says, "I give you the thunder of my silence."

To an unduly mean offender, he replies, "If I were an undertaker or a hangman there is no one I would rather see than you."

And to one who has been inordinately malignant, Celler says, "I believe in birth control, provided that, with respect to you, they make it retroactive."

⟨ The propensity of Senators to talk at great length on subjects for which they admittedly have no answers is a habit "more honored in the breach than in the observance." Early in 1966, Michigan's Philip A. Hart, who is noted for his honorable breach of that custom, gave some insights into the causes of the phenomenon.

"The Record earlier today will show I was present," Hart noted. "Having read my mail, if I did not say a word as this debate closed I would be scolded by those at home who do know the answers, and not all of these knowledgeable persons are at home; some are here . . .

"I do wish that in Congress as well as in this country there would be a little more willingness to be tentative, tentative in our judgments of what the history of the moment requires, tentative in our judgment of the motives of others . . .

"It is unfortunate that a member of this body feels he must rise and say something lest he be clobbered as forfeiting his responsibility. . . ."

❲ During March, 1966, Senator Philip Hart of Michigan sought to reassure manufacturers who were fearful of the impact of the Truth in Packaging Bill; he read into the Congressional Record an article describing the experience of some honest Virginia horse traders, who at one auction experimented with the practice of listing each animal's faults in the sales catalog.

Some of the typical notations follow:

"Maroma: This mare requires an individual paddock." But Maroma nevertheless brought $31,000 seconds after the bidding opened.

"Rose Fern: This mare's foals are subject to jaundice." Rose Fern sold for $77,000.

"Ambernash: Operated on for sesamoids in July, 1965." The price: a hefty $25,000.

"Alto Ribot: This colt has a chronic, injured stifle." He was nevertheless sold for $30,000.

"Virtue," Hart said, "is its own reward. But it's not necessarily the only reward."

❲ Speaking before the American Newspaper Guild Convention in July, 1965, Senator Philip A. Hart of Michigan made a few pungent observations concerning the "power of the press":

"I remember the Presidential campaign of 1948, when Mr. Truman vigorously declared that he was the victim of a Republican-controlled press that was distorting his views and programs and turning the public against him without justification.

"There was, by the way, considerable evidence to support his claim. Of course, in order to prove it conclusively he should have been defeated at the polls.

"He wasn't prepared to go that far, but his charges, I think, proved two things: One, that the press is as thin-skinned about criticism as are politicians. Secondly, that millions of studious Americans were prompted to study the facts themselves before making an evaluation and walking into the polls. It was, I think, a good evaluation of the candidate in question.

"The same thing recurred during the Goldwater campaign. Senator Goldwater charged the press was distorting his views and turning the public against him. Once again, I think, millions of studious Americans studied the facts for themselves and made an evaluation. Once again, I think it was a good evaluation of the candidate in question. . . .

"An editor who publishes a weekly in Frankfort, Michigan, had one view that I remember especially well. During last year's campaign he ran a page-one editorial that spoke approvingly of me and endorsed me for reelection. It wasn't slanted, by the way. It was all true.

"The next week he ran a little story headlined 'Power of the Press,' in which he reported that the day after the previous issue was out, he walked outside to find his thirteen-year-old daughter distributing bumper stickers that read, 'Peterson for U.S. Senate.' . . .

"It's been my observation that most Washington newspapermen—while very capable—tend to be overworked and overextended.

"I also believe that most of them are underpaid. Now there's a test for the objectivity of publishers. Let's see if they print that! . . ."

Then, after having pointed out a few of the press' more unavoidable shortcomings, Hart added, "But enough of that. I think you know what I'm getting at and I don't want to sound like the Mafia chieftain who appeared at the city editor's desk, shifted his shoulders, blew out a puff of cigar smoke, and growled, 'Why don't you ever print the good we do?' . . .

"As to my own case, I think I can honestly say this: newspapermen have made me look better than I am more often than they've made me look worse than I am. And I've never found them short on compassion.

"I have an example: Some time ago, Dave Brady, a sports writer on the Washington *Star*, covered hearings I was conducting on a sports bill. His report mentioned the hearing in passing and then went on to nominate me for the job of Baseball Commissioner—a truly compassionate act.

"After watching me for three days trying to make a living in the United States Senate, this fellow—whom I had barely met—went out and made a real try to get me a respectable job.

"You can't help but like people like that. Thank you."

❲ After six months in Congress, Maryland Representative Hervey G. Machen found that people still could not seem to spell his name correctly in their correspondence with him. He gratefully sent this note to the Post Office in 1965: "I must commend the Post Office Department and Postmaster General Granowsky, er, Grounouskii, that is Groundowzski, or is it Grounouski for the good work in getting the mail to me."

❲ Carl Albert, Democratic majority leader in the House of Representatives, gave a rundown of possible Presidential candidates at the Gridiron dinner in January, 1964:
"Mr. Knebel, President Johnson, Mr. Chief Justice, my

colleagues of the Congress, distinguished members of the press and other writers of fiction, distinguished publishers and other Republicans:

"Mark Twain said that 'the only way for a newspaperman to look at a politician is *down.*' The authors of the last skit took him at his word. They have correctly referred to me as being from Bug Tussle, Oklahoma, but the inference was that that was my only claim to fame. I can tell you that visitors to the House Gallery think otherwise. They think I am a junior page boy.

"This is a most impressive assemblage. As I look at the conglomeration of politicians and reporters, I suggest that it is rare indeed to find both the Saturday afternoon and Monday morning quarterbacks in such harmony and good fellowship—*temporary though it may be.*

"Also, I am happy to welcome back to Washington former Vice-President Nixon—*temporary though it may be.*

"The last skit reminded me of a spectacle in the Coliseum in ancient Rome. The only difference was that—in those days, the *Senators* watched—while the *Christians* were fed to the lions. But it's great fun tonight—for the Christians.

"I assume that one of the reasons I was invited here was to give a report on the status of the Eighty-eighth Congress. This present session is expected to be short. About 2 billion dollars short. There was one advantage in last year's twelve months' session; we didn't have time to go home and explain it to the voters.

"But this year we're moving faster. Did you notice how quickly the Senate wound up the Bobby Baker investigation?

"There have been discussions of major reforms. A lot of people want to do things with the Rules Committee. The smart ones just want to get on it.

"But the one subject everyone is interested in at this

time—is the selection of candidates. Next fall there is to be an election. I guess you know this—it's been in all the papers. On the Democratic side, President Johnson happily goes from day to day, just doing what comes naturally—and 77 per cent of the voters approve. Things are going so well for him that they tell me he opens Cabinet meetings with the prayer that Divine Providence remain under the protection of the Administration.

"You don't have to have a strong President to make free collective bargaining work—but it sure helps.

"President Johnson has already set a new record in five months. He's the first President to operate in the dark on purpose.

"The President has both prosperity and poverty working for him. He has even taken over the middle of the road—from ditch to ditch.

"And, everybody wants to help him. The other day Adlai Stevenson showed up at the White House wearing a western hat and cowboy boots. Bill Moyers whispered to the President, 'I wonder if he's trying to tell us something.'

"On the Republican side, the present situation seems to be mildly confused—and even puzzling. When the voters in New Hampshire were offered their choice between Eastern New York and Western Arizona, they chose South Vietnam.

"I've followed the positions Senator Goldwater has taken these past few months. He's the only bull I ever saw who carries around his own china shop. The Senator refuses to be briefed on foreign affairs—he's just not going to let his campaign get bogged down with any facts.

"In the morning papers I read that Barry claims 525 delegates—this is the first time I've ever known Goldwater to take a liberal position.

"Americans traditionally have admired the self-made man—which brings us to Nelson Rockefeller. He is a man who has risen to immense wealth in just three generations. I understand that Goldwater and Rockefeller have decided to bury the hatchet—*in* Cabot Lodge.

"But Ambassador Lodge is hard to get to. And the longer he stays away, the better the voters like him. If you believe the polls—nothing stands between Lodge and the top of the ladder—except the ladder.

"Also, I don't want to overlook my good friend, former Vice-President Nixon. At a dinner party the other evening, the hostess leaned over to Dick and said, 'You know, Mr. Nixon, I've heard a great deal about you.' 'That's possible,' Dick replied, 'but you can't prove anything.'

"It's a little hard to figure the role of Governor Romney. My opinion is, he's being kept under wraps in case the Republican kingmakers at San Francisco need a stop-Stassen candidate.

"Gridiron Dinners have a certain element in common with an election year. They give us the chance to see ourselves as others see us.

"This decade may present our generation its best opportunity to cover great distances in the world struggle. Today's dawn presents us the disarray in that camp which has opposed a peaceful world. I think we can distinguish a gift from a Trojan Horse. The hazard today is to lose this rare opportunity by being committed to yesterday's battleplans.

"Nothing is going to help us more in this generation than a sense of history—unless it's a sense of humor.

"As I conclude, I cannot miss this opportunity to get in a plug for my party. I say to you, gentlemen, that all my party wants is the chance to complete its program.

"And what is its program?

"To stay in office another four years."

❨ During 1965 Senator Allen J. Ellender of Louisiana told
a convocation of students at Oklahoma City University:

"A seventh-grade student recently wrote me as follows:
'I would appreciate it very much if you would send me
maps, charts, books, posters, papers, pamphlets, folders,
objects, and anything else you think I need to make good
projects and reports on the following topics: the History
and study of North America (since it was made to now, the
Ice Age, how it was formed, how it reacted to different
periods of time, the Indians, the animals, its discovery, how
the government of the land changed under the rule of white
men, etc.), the History of New Orleans (when it was
founded, the battle of New Orleans, as the capital of Louisiana, the port, etc.), the Korean War (the battles in
Korea, in America, how it was fought, why it was fought,
the leaders of the armies and countries, etc.).'

"I have had numerous requests from students asking for
'all the information there is about our government and our
history.'

"There was also the lady who wanted me to stop the gas
company employee from stepping on her flowers every time
he came to read the gas meter.

"A seven-year-old boy wrote and asked me to help him
determine the sex of his pet crow—he said that since I am
Chairman of the Agriculture Committee I should be able to
tell about the sex of crows."

❨ Alabama's Senator John Sparkman tells the story about
his senior colleague, Senator Lister Hill, who once had an
embarrassing run-in with a fellow Senator in the dimly lit
subway connecting the Capitol and the Senate Office Building.

Hill saw the other Senator approaching with a woman
whom he thought he recognized as the man's wife. That

day's session had been particularly wearying, and Hill felt
the need for some playful repartee. "Senator———,"
joked Hill, "if you don't stop running around with this
good-looking woman, I'm going to have to tell your wife."
The woman, of course, was not his wife.

❡ Representative Oren Harris of Arkansas offers this
maxim for Washington people: "Beware of the man who
knows the answer before he understands the question."

❡ During the 1957 hearings before the housing subcommittee of the Senate Committee on Banking and Currency,
the following exchange took place between Senators Paul
Douglas of Illinois and John Sparkman of Alabama:

DOUGLAS: "I understand that some people down there
[Alabama] don't like New Englanders too well."

SPARKMAN: "Oh, that's not so. We have a good many
people in Alabama from New England."

DOUGLAS: "I understand that you refer to them as 'Dam-
yankees.' "

SPARKMAN: "[Quickly] Oh, no! We don't limit the use
of that word just to New Englanders."

❡ Senator Henry M. Jackson of Washington tells the story
about the drunk who approached a passerby and asked him
for the time of day. The passerby told him, whereupon the
drunk mumbled confusedly, "I can't figure it out. All day
long, I get different answers."

❡ Senator Sam Ervin of North Carolina broke up the Senate with this story:

"When I think of the Republican and Democratic platforms, I am reminded of a story which Judge Walter Siler of Chatham County, North Carolina, used to tell about an old couple from Chatham County who went down to Fayetteville, their shopping center, to do their fall shopping.

"In those old days, people traveled by covered wagon. They took one day to drive from Chatham to Fayetteville; they spent the next day shopping; and on the third day, they returned home. They were accustomed to camp out in the open on the hill that overlooks Fayetteville. The old couple, John and Mary, had completed their shopping, and they had gone back up to the campsite, and were waiting for the fire that they had kindled to burn high enough to cook their supper. While they were waiting, Mary checked over some of the bills for the articles she had purchased. She said to her husband, 'John, you know some of those merchants down there in Fayetteville are crooked. They have charged us for a lot of stuff we didn't get. Just look here.'

"She picked up one of the bills and read: 'So many yards of calico, so much; ditto, so much.'

"She said, 'I never bought any ditto. They charged me for something that I didn't get. You get on one of the horses and ride down there and find out about this.'

"So John got on a horse and rode down to Fayetteville. After a time, Mary saw him coming back. She said to John, 'What did you find out?'

"He said, 'Mary, I found out that I'm a damned fool and that you are ditto.' "

❨ Senator Samuel Ervin recounts this story of Francis Garrou, a resident of Valdese, North Carolina, whom Ervin describes as the wisest man that ever lived in that state. "On one occasion, the people of Valdese were preparing to hold a municipal election. They saw fit to put the name of Francis Garrou on the ballot as a candidate for mayor, without his consent.

"One day a cotton broker was in Mr. Garrou's mill before the scheduled municipal election trying to sell him cotton. Mr. Garrou was a very indignant about his name having been presented upon the ballot without his consent, and he said to the cotton broker that if he was elected to the office, he wouldn't qualify.

"The election was held, and after some weeks, the broker returned to Valdese on another visit to sell some cotton to Mr. Garrou. He remembered the conversation he had had with him the last time he was in Valdese, so he asked Mr. Garrou how the municipal election came out.

"Francis Garrou said, 'You know, the fools went ahead and elected me mayor.'

"The cotton broker then asked, 'Mr. Garrou, did you qualify?'

"Francis Garrou said, 'I have been sworn in and cussed out. If that does not qualify a man for public office in the United States, I do not know what does.' "

❡ This excerpt from the Congressional Record provides an example of the way a politician can put his wit to work for him. The scene is the Senate floor during the civil rights debates of 1959, and the speaker is Senator Samuel J. Ervin, Jr., of North Carolina:

"The Attorney General has a criminal statute which he can use. He has a civil statute which he can use. Yet he comes to Congress to ask us to give him a third statute. The Attorney General reminds me of the fellow who went 'a-courtin'.' John was 'a-courtin' ' Mary, and John said to Mary, 'Mary, if you wasn't what you is, what would you

like to be?' Mary said, 'I would like to be an American
beauty rose.' And then she inquired of John. 'John, if you
wasn't what you is, what would you like to be?' And John
said, 'Mary, if I wasn't what I is, I would like to be an
octopus.' Mary said, 'John, what is an octopus?' John said,
'An octopus is sort of a fish that has got a thousand arms.'
Mary said to John, 'Well, now, John, if you was an octopus, what would you do with those thousand arms?'

"And John said, 'Mary, I would put every last one of
them around you.' Mary said to John, 'Go on away from
here, John; you ain't usin' the two arms you've already
got.' [Laughter.]

"The Attorney General of the United States already has
two arms. I assure Senators that either one of them is suffi-
cient to put around any person anywhere in the South who
is willfully denying to any qualified person of any color or
race the right to register or to vote or to have his vote
counted, as cast."

❲ As does every public official, Senator William Proxmire
of Wisconsin occasionally receives a few particularly insult-
ing or annoying letters. Some of his replies—never mailed,
of course—are worth recording.

One constituent asked why the Senator voted for the
education bill. The constituent wrote:

"Although I am in my early thirties I am of the old
school in believing that the American public can do with
less federal aid. We should be made to help ourselves instead of becoming parasites dependent on government
'handouts.'

"In closing I would appreciate receiving a copy of your
Congressional Record."

The Senator replied: "You say you don't want to become a parasite, so I don't think I will send you that copy

of the Congressional Record you asked for. You can go out and buy one."

Another letter, from two fifth-graders, complained about Communist thefts of our nuclear and defense information. "We wondered why a law couldn't be passed to keep Russians out of the United States so they couldn't steal our secrets," they wrote.

The reply: "It so happens we do have a law to keep people out of the United States. It is called the McCarran-Walter Immigration Act, and it keeps not only Communists, but everybody else out of the United States.

"If the Russians get our secrets, then they are going to be two years behind, just like we are."

Another constituent volunteered his views "to serve as a guide in voting." They included opposition to the education bill, the farm program, foreign aid, and eight "etcs."

The Senator wrote: "Most of your views are contrary to mine, but I got elected and you didn't. That's the way the old cookie crumbles, pal."

Another contended, among other things, that the fact that President Eisenhower appointed Earl Warren to the Supreme Court was insufficient proof of Warren's patriotism.

The reply: "If you are still curious about why Mr. Eisenhower appointed Warren, I suggest you write directly to the farm at Gettysburg. In fact, send all your future letters there. Mr. Eisenhower needs a lot of fertilizer these days, so they say."

One letter said, in its entirety: "Please vote against that insidious bill."

The reply: "Tough luck. The Insidious Bill passed last week. I was in favor of it."

⟨ In response to growing concern in 1965 over Congressmen's children holding down government summer jobs that might otherwise have been filled by needy teen-agers, Wisconsin Senator William Proxmire repaid to the U.S. Treasury some $1800 earned by his son and step-daughter during their vacations. However, the children got to keep their money "because they earned it. Besides," added Proxmire, "if you know teen-agers, they don't give back money anyway."

⟨ Senator Russell B. Long of Louisiana loves to retell this classic, a legacy of his father, the memorable Huey Long: "After years of nagging by a pious wife, a whiskey-drinking, card-playing old reprobate finally decided to silence her by joining the Baptist Church. On baptism day, the congregation assembled at the creek bank, sang a few hymns, then watched the old man led into the water.

"As the water came up to his waist, an ace of spades floated out of his back pocket. He waded deeper and out floated a king of spades, then the queen, then the jack and finally a ten. His wife could bear it no longer. 'Stop it!' she shrieked. 'He's lost! He's lost!'

" 'Hold on there, Ma,' interrupted her son, who was standing beside her. 'Paw ain't lost. If he cain't win with that hand, ain't nobody ever gonna win.' "

⟨ Congresswoman Edith Green of Oregon, with her direct feminine logic, cannot understand the Federal Government's spending some 6 million dollars to help tobacco farmers, while simultaneously spending 3 million dollars in proving that cigarettes are dangerous. In fact, she was moved to express her sentiments in verse:

Extensive tests have now
  revealed that smoking is injurious.
I find this notice puzzling,
  in fact, it leaves me curious.
The Congress in its wisdom has enacted legisia-
  tion
To protect us from the dangers of smoke annihila-
  tion.
Tobacco firms must label all—and risks be pub-
  licized,
But by an overwhelming vote, the crops are sub-
  sidized.

❰ South Dakota's Democratic Senator George McGovern made this contribution to the 1966 controversy involving the construction of a permanent residence for the Vice-President: "As for the argument that the United States can't afford to build a Vice-Presidential home, I can only say that this makes little sense. If we can afford an aquarium for the fish in the National Capital, we can surely afford a house for the Vice-President."

❰ Senator Edmund S. Muskie of Maine has some delightful stories about the residents of his state, whose taciturnity is legendary:

"A visitor to New Harbor tried in vain to start a conversation. Finally he asked if the town had a law against talking. 'Not a law,' he was told, 'but we've got an understanding not to say anything unless it improves a silence!'"

"One young salesman had no luck at all selling Joe Kendall an encyclopedia of farming. 'Hell, sonny,' Joe said, 'I'm only farming half as good as I know how to now.'"

"An Oxford County boy without much schooling was asked if he could read. When he answered 'Kinda,' the man asked him what he meant. 'Well, sir,' the boy replied, 'when I get to a crossroad I can tell how far but I can't tell where to.' "

❨ Maine's Democratic Senator Edmund S. Muskie has formulated some guidelines for the proper manner of addressing a colleague in debate: "If you and he are in complete agreement, you address him merely as 'The Senator from such and such a state.'

"If you are not too sure he agrees with you, you should refer to him as 'The able Senator from . . .'

"But if you know there is violent disagreement on an issue, then there is only one way to address him: 'The able and distinguished Senator, my friend from . . .' "

❨ Once, while preoccupied with the costs of campaign finance, Senator Joseph Montoya of New Mexico asked a visitor to his office to sign the "checkbook" instead of the "guestbook."

❨ New Mexico's Senator Joseph Montoya, of Spanish descent, is fluent in the language and proud of New Mexico's Hispanic traditions. While he often complains that his staff is too anglicized, he also acknowledges that they don't need to speak much Spanish because "the word for 'no' is the same in both languages."

❨ The opposition of Southern Senators to proposed civil rights legislation in 1960 led to some fairly brisk debate, which contained its share of humorous repartee. In this exchange Louisiana's Russell B. Long and Illinois' Paul H. Douglas manifest considerable erudition—both Biblical and secular—in addition to ready wit.

LONG: "I hope I can find the quotation from the Sermon on the Mount. I think it so aptly applies to the situation involved in the civil rights case. I do not want to make a mistake in quoting the Bible. I think when we quote Jesus, we ought to try to be accurate about it. I am quoting from the Holy Word itself, Matthew, Chapter 7, the Sermon on the Mount:

> Judge not, that ye be not judged.
> For with what judgment ye judge, ye shall be judged; and with what measure ye mete, it shall be measured to you again.
> And why beholdest thou the mote that is in thy brother's eye, but considerest not the beam that is in thine own eye?

"Mr. President, some folks who may not be Bible readers may not know what a mote is. A mote is a teeny, teeny speck of dust. 'Teeny' means it is almost impossible to see with the naked eye. If a person can see it at all, he is lucky.

"On the other hand, the beam, the other Biblical term referred to, is a fairly good-sized piece of wood, I suppose about the size of a splinter. Jesus said to the people, in his Sermon on the Mount:

> And why beholdest thou the mote—

"this little speck of dust—

> that is in thy brother's eye, but considerest not the beam that is in thine own eye?
> Or how wilt thou say to thy brother—

"Jesus goes on to say:

> Or how wilt thou say to thy brother, Let me pull out the mote out of thine eye, and, behold, a beam is in thine own eye?
> Thou hypocrite—

"That is not addressed to any Senator; that is Jesus talking to the people in general—

> Thou hypocrite, first cast out the beam out of thine own eye; and then shalt thou see clearly to cast out the mote out of thy brother's eye.

"The Senators from New York State tell us that we ought to do something about four little parishes in Louisiana where twenty thousand colored persons do not qualify as voters. Yet in their own state of New York there are 618,000 Puerto Ricans who cannot qualify because the laws of the state prohibit them from doing so.

"Jesus said:

> Thou hypocrite, first cast out the beam out of thine own eye, and then shalt thou see clearly to cast out the mote out of thy brother's eye.

"In other words, let New York State first take care of its 618,000 Puerto Ricans. After New York has done that, she will be better able to tell the folks in Louisiana how to deal with four little river parishes where twenty thousand colored folks live."

DOUGLAS: "I have been greatly impressed with the Biblical knowledge exhibited and the evangelical discourse given by my great friend from Louisiana in quoting from the sayings of Jesus. But I think the Senator also realizes, does he not, that Jesus did not say, 'Thou shalt not cast the beam out of thine eye because there is a mote in thine eye'?"

LONG: "No. The Senator is quite correct. Jesus said, 'First cast out the beam out of thine own eye.' One had to do that first. That is what I am trying to tell the Senator.

"Look; here is the Civil Rights Commission's report. I did not have anything to do with it. I did not even vote for it. Senators stood here and fought this thing for months, and forced some of us to submit ourselves to it. We did not approve of it.

"Look what this commission said about Chicago, from whence comes the distinguished Senator from Illinois.

"I skip a couple of paragraphs, and find it says:

> The general metropolitan residential pattern shows Chicago . . . on the basis of census maps, to be the most residentially segregated city in America.

"Imagine that. We have an area where they say segregation is evil, and the largest city up there, the second largest city in the entire United States, is said to be the most segregated city in America. Look at the map, and there it is. Some persons talk about segregated schools. That is what they have in Chicago."

DOUGLAS: "The segregation which does exist in Chicago is not a legal segregation. People are free to live as they wish, and though there is opposition to Negroes moving into white neighborhoods, they are accorded police protection. The segregation which exists in many of our southern states—and I am not indicting the South—is a legal segregation, and there is a great deal of difference between these two types of segregation."

LONG: "Mr. President, I wish I could quote the language, which I learned from the Senator from Illinois, the distinguished scholar and student, who tells us of the magnificent impartiality of the law, which prevents princes and paupers alike from sleeping under bridges and permits them to walk in the rain for lack of shelter."

DOUGLAS: "Mr. President, the Senator is more an expert on the Bible than he is on the writings of Anatole France. The quotation which I gave was from Anatole France's novel *The Red Lily*, which speaks of the majestic equality of the laws, which prohibit the rich as well as the poor from sleeping under bridges and begging in the streets for bread."

LONG: "I am glad the Senator quoted correctly, because I want it for the Record. The point I am getting to is this: Look at Chicago; look at it. Look where the colored men live, and look where the white people live. The colored go to segregated schools; there are nobody but colored folks in the schools, because they keep all the colored in the same areas."

DOUGLAS: "Mr. President, I must protest. We do not keep Negroes in segregated districts. They are free legally to move."

LONG: "They just cannot get there. [Laughter.] What I am trying to say is this: If segregation is evil, why do you practice it in Chicago?"

DOUGLAS: "Mr. President, may I make a reply? It so happens, in the section of Chicago in which my wife and I live, that about 50 per cent of the persons who reside in that area are Negroes, and that in the public school which is nearest to our apartment, the students are perhaps 60 per cent Negroes.

"It is an integrated community. I frankly admit that over the years that this has been happening, we have had our difficulties. But we have carried through with it. We believe we shall be successful in it. And the relationships between the races are much better than they would have been if we had used either force or the pressure of law to maintain it as an all-white community."

LONG: "All I did was read the report.

"It asks where segregation exists. It says more is found in

the second largest city in the country—Chicago. And the report also describes the practices in New York.

"I think the Senator will be fair enough to admit that in most instances the colored children in Chicago are going to schools in the areas shown in black on the map, where the schools are practically confined to Negro children.

"Mr. President, I have had occasion to speak to people from various large cities who tell us how the school-board members gerrymander the school districts, so that almost all the white children attend white schools, and almost all the colored children attend colored schools, Negro schools.

"But the Good Book tells us that Jesus said:

> Thou hypocrite, first cast out the beam out of thine own eye; and then shalt thou see clearly to cast out the mote out of thy brother's eye."

DOUGLAS: "Well——"

LONG: "Mr. President, I have not been quoting any remarks by the Senator from Illinois. I have been quoting what Jesus said, as it is recorded in the Bible, in the Book of Matthew."

DOUGLAS: "But I remind the Senator from Louisiana that he should worry more about removing the beam from his own eye."

LONG: "But, Mr. President, I have not urged the enactment of five pounds of bills, in an effort to tell someone else how to run his own business."

❲ While serving as chairman of the Senate aviation subcommittee, Senator A. S. "Mike" Monroney visited the U.S. Air Force Academy. Asking his guide the meaning of the academy's seventeen spires, he received this reply: "This is supposed to be an official Air Force secret, Senator. But the seventeen spires represent the twelve apostles and the five members of the subcommittee."

❨ Speaking at a gathering of the Rockland County Democrats in Nyack, New York, in 1965, Senator Ralph Yarborough made these remarks:

"In honor of this being a dinner-dance tonight, I have chosen to entitle my speech 'Democratic Party A Go-Go.' I thought this was appropriate for several reasons: First, the Democratic Party is a party of the times. From Franklin D. Roosevelt, Harry Truman, John F. Kennedy, and now my fellow Texan Lyndon B. Johnson, the Democratic Party has shown that you can't run a fast-paced nation to the beat of the minuet. In modern terms, we could describe the progress made under the Democratic Party as 'swinging.'

"The Democratic Party, like our contemporary discotheques, has upped the tempo of progress, been an economic success, and gotten the people off their seats and started them moving. Under Democratic leadership, the country has gone from 'stagnant to stereo,' and the sounds of progress are reaching to all corners of this great nation of ours.

"This year alone, we have passed an unparalleled amount of the President's Great Society program. Rather than stand still as another party advocates, the Democratic Party is a party of ideas—you might say that we are not afraid to add a new 'twist' to the progress of this nation.

"The Democratic Party is working, progressing, moving —we are in the 'swim' of things in this country. We have become so renowned that there is even a new dance called the 'Mule,' which I am sure was named after the donkey symbol for the Democratic Party."

5. The Wits of the Great Society

⟨ THIS SECTION is devoted to the Cabinet members and other appointed officials of the Johnson Administration, in addition to a certain few perennial Washington observers whose stature entitles them to a place in this anthology. While each appointee brings to his office a distinctive brand of humor, as a group these officials tend to represent the true flavor and tenor of any given administration. Of special interest in this area is the growth of the public role of the press secretary, a subject to which Bill Moyers devoted an entire speech.

Contrary to what might be expected, the higher one goes in government circles, the more prevalent is a good sense of humor and a readiness to enjoy a good laugh. This phenomenon would seem to demonstrate that wit is not merely an adjunct to a politician's stock of weapons and tools, but rather an indispensable element in his over-all personality.

❲ Secretary of State Dean Rusk was reportedly itemizing his expense account after his 1963 conferences in Costa Rica: "Breakfast, $2.95; lunch with two foreign ministers, $4,000,000 . . ."

❲ Senator John Williams of Delaware was mildly reproving Secretary of State Dean Rusk for not sticking closely to a question put to him at a Senate Foreign Relations Committee hearing in 1964.

"When I was young up here on Capitol Hill," countered Rusk, "I was told, 'If you can't answer the question, answer another one.' "

❲ Secretary of State Dean Rusk was filling out an official federal employment form, when he paused at the line that asked whether any of his relatives had ever plotted the overthrow of the United States Government. After some consideration, Georgia-born Rusk wrote, "My two grandfathers."

Both had served in the Confederate Army.

❲ Secretary of State Dean Rusk capsulized the situation at the height of the 1962 Cuban missile crisis: "We're eyeball to eyeball and I think the other fellow just blinked."

❲ During March, 1965, Dean Rusk cited an example of how the State Department was following the Administration's economy guidelines: "Three years ago," he said, "Congress said we couldn't have any more people. Last year I didn't even ask for any more, and this year the President said I'd have to get along with fewer people."

"This shows," added the Secretary of State, "that it is not just dogs that get their ears pulled in Washington."

❨ At a cocktail party in October, 1965, Soviet Foreign Minister Gromyko asked Secretary of State Dean Rusk if Congress was currently in session. Rusk replied that it was and that its present topic of debate was home rule for the District of Columbia. Cracked the Secretary of State, "It's one of our last vestiges of colonialism."

❨ Suggested Secretary of State Dean Rusk in 1961, "Perhaps the United States has reached the point where we must not act like an old cow who is supposed simply to accept kicks in the flanks rather placidly, but rather, we must begin to show our horns a little bit."

❨ During a Washington meeting of Harvard Law School Alumni, Secretary of Labor Willard Wirtz (Harvard Law '37) recommended this sample line for an ambitious New Frontiersman leaving a cocktail party early: "I have to get back to my office and meet the staff. Evenings are the only time we can get together."

A couple of evenings thereafter, Wirtz was working late at the office when he received a call on his private phone. "Just checking," the anonymous caller said, and hung up.

❨ In remarks before the Civil Rights Commission during November, 1965, Secretary of Labor Willard Wirtz related the story of an experience he had with one unemployed youth. Wirtz asked the unkempt young man, "What kind of work do you want?"

"Anything that pays decent," replied the high school dropout.

"What is decent?" asked Wirtz.

Answered the youth, "Oh, about 70–75–80."

"I thought he meant cents-per-hour," noted the Secretary of Labor. "When I found he was talking about dollars-a-week, I thought of the older wisdom that people who want by the yard but try by the inch ought to be kicked by the foot."

❦ Secretary of Labor Willard Wirtz spoke before the Civil Rights Conference in Washington in November, 1965:

"Oliver Wendell Holmes used to tell of the instructions he was given for a dinner at which he was to speak. 'What we like,' the chairman told him, 'is to gather, gobble, gabble, and git—in that order and about that fast.'

"I am under similar instructions tonight. I have been told bluntly that this is not a conference for bureaucrats; that it is a convening rather of 'the best minds in the country'—with the plain implication that none of them works for the government. 'Your appearance,' I was advised, 'will be on a separate but equal basis, and you will proceed to your conclusion with all deliberate speed.'

"A firm believer in cloture, I have agreed to say nothing this evening that could possibly be misconstrued as bearing on the conference subject."

❦ Addressing the "Plans for Progress Fourth National Conference" in January, 1966, Secretary of Labor Willard Wirtz was discussing discrimination of various kinds:

"There is also the matter of discrimination between men

and women. We have just completed a survey of some 1,500 collective bargaining agreements, most of which contain some provisions differentiating between men and women. Some of them are natural enough. I find no basis for calling out the troops because some of these contracts include maternity-leave provisions. No distinction or discrimination, at least, involved there."

⟨ In October, 1965, Secretary of Labor Willard Wirtz opened a press conference with these remarks: "Good morning. I have a headful of cold. I am sorry it isn't operable, and you will just have to put up with the difficulties that it presents."

⟨ In August, 1965, Secretary of Labor Willard Wirtz spoke at the launching of the USS *George Washington Carver* at Newport News, West Virginia: "The man whose spirit presides here today would have left out this part of these ceremonies, for he despised speeches; either making them, or—worse—hearing them. 'You have never,' he said once, 'seen a heavy thinker with his mouth open.' I shall speak briefly."

⟨ In March, 1966, Bill Moyers, Press Secretary to President Johnson, spoke before the National Newspaper Association on the subject of the role of the Press Secretary, its frustrations and its rewards. Reprinted here almost in full, his eloquent address amply demonstrates that true wit encompasses far more than humor, although humor certainly abounds here. But informing this humor is a first-rate intellect, a mind not only of considerable learning, but also of incisive critical insight.

"For more than one reason I am glad to be here. (It's good to get away from—the White House—press corps.)

"At the last minute the President changed his schedule rather suddenly and I almost had to cancel. He has a way of doing that. Not too long ago he called me and said, 'Bill, I'm going to Honolulu.' I said, 'Fine, Mr. President, I'll come over and talk to you about it. Where are you?' He said, 'Over Los Angeles.'

"A number of factors compound the frustration of my work, two more so than others: the President and the press.

"The credibility gap is a problem, too. It is getting so bad we can't even believe our own leaks. There have been so many leaks we are stamping our morning newspapers 'TOP SECRET.'

"And then there are planted questions. Every press secretary has dealt with planted questions, but I have moved on to planted answers. The President gives the answer and we let the reporters guess the question. Of course, as I said, the object of planted questions is to make sure the American people get the real news—not just what is on some reporter's mind.

"I have only been in this job eight months. It took me only eight hours to learn that it is good for a Press Secretary to keep his words soft and sweet—because he never knows when he will have to eat them.

"This job changes you. Someone anonymously sent me a quotation with a note attached saying: 'This is very appropriate for you.' It read: 'One is more honest in youth, and to the age of thirty, than when he has passed it. It is only after that age that one's illusions are dispelled. Until then, one resembles the dog that defends the dinner of his master against other dogs; after this period, he takes his share of it with the others.' At the end, my anonymous benefactor had written: 'Arf! Arf!'

"I guess that metamorphosis is a kind of occupational

hazard. Earlier this week a former journalist who has been reduced to writing letters to the editor penned one note to a local newspaper in which he tabbed me with a new name: 'Common Scold.' And that was after he had described me as 'a reformed divinity student who now seems determined to play the role of a nagging wife.'

"Today I want neither to scold nor to nag, but to talk to you as an ex-newspaperman of limited experience who has sought to add to his knowledge with some intensive on-the-job training.

"I have made a few tentative observations in the last eight months on the virtues and vices of Press Secretaries. I emphasize 'tentative' because in this town only the most dogmatic dares accept as final any conclusion embraced on the basis of available evidence at any given moment.

"Six years ago I came to Washington as a kind of irreverent believer. Today I suppose I could be called a reverent skeptic—reverent because the stakes of what we are all doing are too high for superficial playacting; skeptic because, in the final analysis, we are all—the best and the worst of us—playactors. If there is a contradiction in that posture, it is because truth in this city almost always rises from the clash of contradictions.

"These observations I have generously decided to share with you today, not because the White House press corps is intolerant of any views other than those of the Highest Authority, but because you are a captive audience. And there is still in me enough of the parish elocutionist not to let a group like this go without first endowing you with the wisdom of the ages—all thirty-one of them.

"I raise the subject of virtues and vices because as a Protestant I believe in public confession, and in the presence of such an unholy audience, it behooves me to practice a bit.

"Of the former, I shall be brief. The best that you can

say about the role of the Press Secretary is that while it is hell to be both a philosopher and a flak, it is also unique. Not since Moses scribbled on a slab of granite while the Almighty dictated has the role of Amanuensis been accorded so exalted a position in the society of men. The office that has evolved from Joseph Tumulty posting on an office door the daily list of Woodrow Wilson's visitors to Bill Moyers describing Lyndon Johnson's incision as 'long enough,' is the invention of necessity. Gone forever, alas, are the days of Andrew Johnson's Administration when a young reporter, Henry Adams, describing his arrival in Washington, said: 'The first step, of course, was making of acquaintance and the first acquaintance was naturally the President, to whom an aspirant to the press officially paid respect.'

. . .

"But if Moses recorded the Ten Commandments, he also broke them. And so, the vices. The first [to] which press secretaries are susceptible is an affliction known as 'Potomac Fever,' which causes one to swell without growing. This is far more dangerous than hammertoes (and far more common), for it tempts press secretaries down many a crooked path. It can guide us, for example, into unquestioning certitude, even righteousness, in the defense of officialdom. Or it can encourage us to dig redoubts for an Administration's policies instead of searching for fresh perspectives to appraise whether what we are doing is being done well—or ought even to be done at all. The first casualty of righteousness—whether in the First, Second, Third, or Fourth Estate—is always that critical faculty which protects us—and our policies—from absolutism.

" 'Potomac Fever' can produce a bloated sensation—particularly in the area of the ego—that causes Press Secretaries to take themselves much too seriously. There are many symptoms of this, including hypervexation over the annoyances any reporter—especially the pathological troublemakers—can generate; myopia, which blurs their vision of things afar; and the tiger-in-the-tank syndrome manifested by supercharged reaction to criticism, justified and unjustified.

"Soon after I took this job a friend presented to me a framed copy of Lord Macmillan's paragraph: 'If you think of it, it seems a strange and ironical arrangement that when the country has entrusted to a particular group of men the arduous and delicate task of conducting the business of the nation, we at the same time permit them to be harassed by every form of obstruction and vituperation. It is as if we had employed a surgeon to perform a delicate operation and had then arranged that his elbow should be jogged at the most critical moment.'

"It sounded nice, so I hung it on the wall of my study. Not long ago my attention meandered to it for the first time in months and I began to read it over—and over. And then I took it down. We are not surgeons, but stewards. And every man's elbow needs to be jogged if it rests too long on the top of the table. Voltaire warned that a 'sovereign is called a tyrant who knows no law but his caprice,' and if you will scratch most of us lightly, you will uncover at least the inclinations of a bush-league tyrant.

"Overheating has other effects, too, and has even been known to keep press secretaries in voluntary bondage to the grist mill when the baker's shelves are full. Or, put another way, press secretaries may choose the safe way of mastering the jots and tittles of supplying the press with its mechanical needs rather than hazard the uncertain depths of dialogue with the press. This is regretful for both the press and the Press Secretary, although each must share the burden for the demise of dialogue. . . . There is a certain unperturbable security about a charade, but a genuine encounter on public policy accepts no bounds to its risks because only when everything is ventured is anything attained.

"Let me speak of one more affliction common to the lot of press secretaries. It is known as 'Montezuma's Revenge' after the great Aztec publicist who opened Mexico to Spanish tourists. You know what it is; it led someone to remark that every press secretary approaches his job with an open mouth. I learned the hard way that there are times when we cannot—in the words of one of your former colleagues—'permit the priorities of the press to hustle the procedures of government.' I have also learned that it is far better to remain silent and appear uninformed than to speak up and remove all doubt.

"What is the cure for this affliction? A little mental Scotch Tape from time to time and a little more defiance of the temptation to worry about the credibility gap. For one thing, too much talk can increase that breach. Events can make a lie out of the most genuine promises—and the most unequivocal assertions. There is a season for everything, including silence. To equate one's responsibility as the President's spokesman with the necessity to speak on every occasion is, I repeat, to stuff raw meat down the yawning maw of the credibility gap.

"As Chamfort wrote, 'Nearly all men are slaves for the same reason the Spartan assigned for the servitude of the Persians: lack of power to pronounce the syllable NO. To be able to utter that word,' he went on, 'and to live alone, are the only two means to preserve one's freedom and one's character.' I might add that they are also the way to keep Presidents out of trouble not of their own making.

"The real test in the final analysis is whether we are willing to stand on the substance of what our Administration does as the press finds and sees it—and as the people judge it. As far as that judgment is concerned, verbal extremism in the liberty of our defense will be no virtue.

"Somewhere between good reporting and fatuous apologetics, therefore, a press secretary must take his stand—nearer the former if he is courageous and fortunate and sneers at veneration; closer to the latter if he is intoxicated with his own importance or the infallibility of his chief's mortality.

"Wherever he stands, there will be tension. For his calling is daily to disprove the axiom that 'No man can serve two masters.' If he does well, he serves neither all of the time and both most of the time.

"You can see the irony here, because the masters a press secretary serves are by nature protagonists. Arthur Krock of *The New York Times* summed it up:

> Our [the press'] obligations are merely these in deciding whether to go into print with information: Is it true? Has it been legitimately acquired? Is it fit to print—public property or a private matter? These satisfactorily settled, the facts are ready for their bath of printer's ink.
>
> But the statesman has other considerations. Is it premature? Will publication make the going more difficult? Will publication tend to confuse, rather than clarify, the popular mind? These are some of the problems before him, particularly if he is President of the United States in a catastrophic hour, forcing the innermost fibers of his body and the full resources of his spirit into his colossal task.

"The irony is deeper because truth is generated by encounter as fire is made by rubbing together two sticks, and the encounter between these protagonists has often been intensely personal.

"I will illustrate by declassifying some material and reading from a report on a violent outburst at a cabinet meeting. It was precipitated when someone mentioned a newspaper attack on the President. One of the men present later wrote:

> The President was much inflamed, got into one of those passions when he cannot command himself, ran on much on the personal abuse which has been bestowed on him, defied any man on earth to produce one single act of his since he had been in the government which was not done on the purest motives, that he had never repented but once his having slipped the moment of resigning his office, and that was every moment since, that by god he had rather be on his farm than to be made emperor of the world—and yet they were charging him with wanting to be king. That that rascal [the newspaper editor] sent him three of his papers every day, as if he thought he would become the distributor of his papers, that he could see in this nothing but an impudent design to insult him. He ended in his high tone. . . .

"So wrote Thomas Jefferson of George Washington.

"What had been said of our first President? That he violated the Constitution, that he was 'treacherous,' 'mischievous,' 'inefficient.' That he was guilty of 'ostentatious professions of piety,' of 'pusilanimous neglect,' of 'little passions,' 'ingratitude,' 'want of merit,' and 'spurious fame.'

"Of course his response was ferocious, predictable and understandable. Few human beings, and still fewer Presidents, are immune to what Edmund Burke called 'the presumptuous judgment of the ignorant' upon their designs. (The sensitivity of Presidents to criticism, I have observed, is matched only by the sensitivity of the press to criticism. As one of your colleagues recently told me with a smile, 'We can give it but we are against taking it.') We all are. Reality and common sense dictate no alternative but living with criticism, rejecting it when unwarranted, accepting it when reasonable, ignoring it when possible.

"For both the President and the press, in the last analysis, know that each holds a peculiar public trust. The Presidency, after all, was created by the Constitution and the press protected by it. On each that document confers responsibility and privilege. (When we in the Government exercise the right of free speech and are critical of the press, it may often be for reasons of pique, but it is also because we know how important reporting is and how much is lost when like us, you have missed the mark!)

"The Presidents I know, and those I have studied, for all the pain afflicted upon them by the press, come back to the conviction once expressed by Thomas Jefferson. The Prussian minister, visiting Jefferson in his office, saw an opposition paper on his desk, attacking Jefferson viciously. He protested, 'Mr. President, why do you permit such libels?'

"Jefferson replied, 'Put that paper in your pocket, Baron. And should you ever hear the reality of our liberty, the freedom of our press questioned, show them this paper—and tell them where you found it.'

"Enough for one master. What can I say of the first I serve, the Presidency? It defies simple definition, for its full meaning baffles its critics and eludes its observers who must interpret the Official but, like its occupant, can never freely grasp it. As Clinton Rossiter has pointed out, if the Presidency could speak, it would say with Walt Whitman:

> Do I contradict myself?
> Very well then I contradict myself.
> (I am large. I contain multitudes.)

"The Presidency is a place where power and purpose are wonderfully met. On its occupant are heaped the hopes and aspirations of a people's finest nature—and the fears and suspicions of their worst. In a world in which power is our lot, the Presidency 'stands across the path of those who mistakenly assert that democracy must fail because it can neither decide promptly nor act vigorously.' That office is occupied now by a man with a talent for power. If he fails, we all fail. If he succeeds, we all succeed. He is a man who has said that the office he holds 'has made every man who occpuied it, no matter how small, bigger than he was; and no matter how big, not big enough for its demands.' "

⟨ Asked to say grace before a White House dinner, Press Secretary Bill Moyers spoke so softly that he could scarcely be heard. "Speak up, Bill!" bellowed Johnson. "Speak up!"
    "I wasn't addressing you, Mr. President," replied Moyers.

⟨ Noticing Bill Moyers' soft twang, a television interviewer in 1964 queried, "Do I detect a Texas accent?" Retorted Moyers, "Not only in my speech, sir, but in my heart."

⟨ One of Lyndon Johnson's secretaries undertook a campaign in 1965 to preserve the President's artifacts for posterity. Press Secretary Moyers refused to cooperate in the saving of assorted memoranda, jottings, doodlings, and the like. The secretary grew peevish, and, to appease her, Moyers presented her with a bulging brown envelope. It contained chicken bones. Explained Moyers, significantly, "That's what he had for lunch."

⟨ When asked how he had met his spouse, Press Secretary Bill Moyers related, "I met my wife the first day of school at North Texas State University. . . . She sat in front of me. Instead of dropping a handkerchief for me to pick up, she left her books underneath the seat. The professor suggested that I return them to her, and I have been the victim of that conspiracy ever since."

❲ Presidential Press Secretary Bill Moyers admits that he sometimes plants questions during the President's news conferences. Here is a hypothetical question-and-answer session which Moyers composed for some future date:

"Q. Mr. President, would you tell us why you consider a free press essential to the working of our democracy?"

"A. (A long silence, followed by the next question.)"

In reference to accusations that President Johnson's Honolulu conference early in 1966 was timed to obscure the headlines of the Senate Foreign Relations Committee hearings on Vietnam, Moyers imagined this exchange:

"Q. Mr. President, Senator Fulbright resumes his hearings on Vietnam tomorrow. Would you comment?

"A. Well, of course we favor full and open debate on our national policies. . . . Oh, by the way, I'm sending Hubert Humphrey in a rocket to the moon tomorrow."

❲ A Senate hearing was held to determine Bill Moyers' qualifications for the office of Deputy Director of the Peace Corps. At one point Moyers was asked his age, and he replied, "Twenty-eight and a half."

❲ During a Senate hearing concerning his nomination for the post of Deputy Director of the Peace Corps, Bill Moyers was asked if he were not a relation of President Johnson "by blood, marriage, or otherwise."

Answered Moyers, "Only political."

❡ Bill Moyers once addressed a group of Peace Corps volunteers who had returned from their tour of duty and enjoined them to "pursue the ideals of a Joan of Arc with the political prowess of an Adam Clayton Powell."

❡ During the 1964 Presidential campaign, Lyndon Johnson reportedly discharged one of his political "advance men" for making a pass at a young woman who was a member of the staff. A farewell party was held for the man, during which Press Secretary Bill Moyers presented him with a picture of the President, autographed by Moyers and bearing the following inscription: "To ————, who made one advance too many."

❡ Speaking before the annual Radio-Television Correspondents Association dinner in 1966, White House Press Secretary Bill Moyers reported this fictional conversation between him and President Johnson:

LBJ: "Bill, we ought to have a televised press conference."

BM: "But, Mr. President, we had one last year."

LBJ: "Well, it's time for another. Let's have one tomorrow morning."

BM: "We can't do that, Mr. President, the Senate Foreign Relations Committee is on every morning, and we can't upstage them."

LBJ: "Let's have it in the early evening, just when everyone is getting home from work."

BM: "That's when Huntley and Brinkley are on, and you don't want to upstage them."

LBJ: "What's wrong with having it Friday night at 10?"

BM: "That is when *The Man From UNCLE* is on."

LBJ: "Bill, you are going to force me to make Lady Bird buy NBC."

BM: "Not that, Mr. President! She can't own all three!"

❨ Mrs. Elizabeth Carpenter, Press Secretary to Lady Bird Johnson, addressed these remarks to the New York Chapter of the Public Relations Society of America, early in 1966:

"Well, it's great to be in John Lindsay's hometown—the fun city. Good ole accident-prone John! He came down to Washington last week and told us about his troubles. He's been mayor only three months. The lights have gone off. The subways stopped running. The water shortage got worse!

"To quote Mayor Lindsay: 'Nobody's perfect.'

"He may not have everything going for him as mayor. But, one sunny Sunday—and he is the seventh draft choice of the New York Jets.

"We can't say he's not trying. When he was in Washington for the Gridiron dinner, he told us he has a new solution to the water problem. 'My slogan will be,' he said, 'Shower with a friend.'

"Well, here I am, fresh from Washington, which Adlai Stevenson once called 'the city of alcohol, protocol and Geritol.' But it is never short on advice. I consulted some of my friends in the White House on what I should talk about to this illustrious audience. They had a great variety of topics.

"Jack Valenti suggested, 'War and Pizza.' Secretary McNamara thought a good subject would be, 'Let Saigons be Saigons.' The White House physician, Dr. Burkley, offered 'Death is Nature's Way of Telling Us to Slow Down.'

"Bill Moyers said a good subject would be—one he is

very familiar with in handling the press—'How to Give Mouth-to-Mouth-Resuscitation Without Becoming Emotionally Involved.'

"And how could I do without the advice of Dean Rusk. He gave me the best subject—'What to Do in Case of Peace.' "

. . .

"Kerryn King, of course, told me not to worry about today. He said he would provide me with a large potted palm and a friendly audience. I told him what I really needed was a friendly palm and a potted audience.

"Anyway, I have always wanted to come to a long martini lunch in New York. I thank you for the cocktails we had earlier. You really are a tight little organization.

"And I want to congratulate you all on the magnificent job you are doing. I'm not going to tell YOU what you've been doing because you KNOW what you've been doing and it has been magnificent, hasn't it?

"To me, you in the public relations world are a symbol of our nation's greatness. I'm interested in what you stand for, and down in Washington—you've had to stand for quite a lot. You can't say we in government are idle. Wonderous things happen—Secretary of the Treasury, Joe Fowler, puts the frug into frugality—Senator Fulbright is hawking doves. Vice-President Humphrey is also on the wing. He's been traveling so much that when anyone says 'Muriel,' he thinks 'cigars.'

"The new budget IS the highest in history, but it has to cover so many things: the war in Vietnam, the war against poverty, hairnets for Senator Dirksen, insulated swimming suits for our Ambassador to Spain.

"All of us are trying to help the President economize—even in saving electricity. At the White House, we work hard, but we try to cram it all in daylight hours. After all, we'd rather curse the darkness than light one candle.

"Millions are going for the war on poverty. Even the Republicans among us can't complain about that. At least it's being spent on a country we've heard about.

"If you think I'm being partisan, I want to make it clear from the beginning that I believe in the two-party system. I believe in Democrats being the Majority Party and the Republicans being the Minority Party.

"Mr. King said you might like to hear something about my job and the kind of press queries we get. While Bill Moyers worries about Vietnam and de Gaulle, I give my best to dogs, daughters, and delphinium.

"If you think people aren't interested in those subjects, I'll be glad to have you answer my telephone. One of the busiest days and nights was when the White House chef, René Verdon, resigned. There was a lot of speculation as to why René packed up his saucepans and left. It wasn't that René couldn't cook chili. It was that flaming brandy he poured over it that finally got us.

"In addition to chef problems, the President's beagles get wide coverage. We had barely gotten rid of twenty-one hamsters when we found ourselves with five beagle pups. The dogs had nothing to do with Mrs. Johnson's tree planting activity. That is self-liquidating."

⟪ Mrs. Lyndon Johnson's Press Secretary Elizabeth Carpenter once explained why she favors traveling by train rather than by plane: "In my heart I have always known that the Wright brothers were wrong."

⟪ Press Secretary Carpenter, addressing the 1966 Radio-Television Correspondents Association dinner, had this new twist for an old line: "Certainly, you in the industry know that behind every successful radio-TV correspondent stands a woman. And behind her stands his wife!"

❨ Secretary of Agriculture Orville Freeman notes, "The Lord created man with two ends—one to sit on, the other to think with. The future of the world depends on which he chooses—heads, he wins; tails, he loses."

❨ Secretary of Agriculture Orville Freeman observes that "behind every successful man stands a surprised mother-in-law," and also that "behind every successful man stands a wife that tells him what to do and a secretary who does it."

❨ During 1966 Secretary of Agriculture Orville Freeman remarked that long exposure to Vice-President Humphrey's legendary energy had convinced him that the Vice-President must have eaten all the vitamin tablets in his father's South Dakota drugstore . . . and washed them down with a missile-fuel chaser.

❨ When speaking before outdoor groups, Secretary of Agriculture Orville Freeman frequently observes, "The Lord created the world two-thirds water and one-third land, with the obvious intention that man should spend two-thirds of his time fishing and one-third working."

❨ Secretary of the Interior Stewart Udall attributes this story to the late Senator Robert Kerr: "This concerns the four boys whose father died, and they were sitting down and discussing matters, and they all agreed that the father had been very fine to all of them, that he had provided well for them, and so on. One of the boys suggested, 'Well, just to be sure that when he goes over on the other side he takes a little money with him, why don't we all—just as a gesture —put some money in the coffin? Let's all put in $125 and let's give him something in case he needs it to go on.'

"All the boys agreed to do this.

"So they went out and came back later and went in individually, and the three first boys put an envelope on their father's coffin. The fourth brother, who was a little sharper, came along and took the three envelopes and wrote out a check and put it in."

《 Secretary of the Interior Stewart Udall delivered one of his favorite jokes before the Women's National Democratic Club during 1961: "The story is that when Khrushchev was here on one of his unlamented visits—I think it was in 1958—he was traveling in San Francisco. There was brought forward to him a Russian who had immigrated to this country a few years ago, and Khrushchev conversed with him.

"He said, 'How do you get along in this factory? How do these capitalists treat you?'

"The man said, 'Very fine. I get along fine.'

"He said, 'Well, what do you mean? How do they deal with their employees? Don't they push you about?'

" 'No, no,' the Russian immigrant said. 'You are walking home and the boss drives by in his big car and picks you up and takes you home.'

"Khrushchev said, 'Really?'

"The immigrant said, 'Yes.'

"He said, 'Again you are walking home. He picks you up and takes you out to dinner in his car and takes you home.'

" 'And,' he added, 'later on, he may stop and pick you up and take you to dinner, and then take you to his home. And you stay at his home overnight.'

"Khrushchev, by then, was quite amazed. He said, 'Really? How often does this happen?'

"The fellow said, 'Well, it has never happened to me, but it happened several times to my sister.' "

⟨ During a speech to the National Rivers and Harbors Congress in May, 1961, Secretary of the Interior Stewart Udall explained, "Any time a new administration come in, you know, you try to get your feet on the ground. So you reach out into industry and also get some of the old retreads from previous administrations and bring people in that you call consultants. Then you have consultants all over the lot.

"Someone asked what a consultant was. I heard a pretty good story the other day of the definition of a consultant. The story was about a young girl in an Eastern college who went out West to spend a summer at a ranch and she began asking questions about the farm animals and the way things took place. She began to ask the cowboys one day what a gelding was. They all passed her off and did not give her an answer. Finally she got one old cowboy off in a corner and asked.

" 'How does a gelding horse differ from other horses?'

"He pawed the ground a little bit and said finally, 'Well, ma'am, a gelding is a horse that runs with the herd, but on a consulting basis only.' "

⟨ Secretary of the Interior Stewart Udall recalls this excerpt from a press conference held in September 1962:

QUESTION: "Can you give us your personal impression

in meeting with Mr. Khrushchev? Mr. Frost has called him rough and ready."

SECRETARY UDALL: "Well, I think the American people are familiar with his personality. I will say to you also that he has a very lively sense of humor. I will tell you one story. He asked the group I was with if I wanted to have my picture taken with him and I answered that I would. And just as the fellow was about to snap the picture, he said, 'If it will help you out, you can go ahead and shake your finger in my face.' So he is quite earthy and human as that would indicate."

⟨ Word play is one of former Postmaster General J. Edward Day's specialties. When Willard Wirtz received his appointment as Secretary of Labor, Day, whose father, Dr. James Day, had performed the delivery of Wirtz' wife, Jane, remarked, "The Day family have been making deliveries for a long time, and the Wirtzes understand what labor is all about."

⟨ As Postmaster General under President Kennedy, J. Edward Day received a multitude of letters requesting positions or advancements, but one in particular seemed to Day the height of audacity. An officer of a large insurance firm wrote, "My wife's cousin's husband who is a dentist would like to be postmaster of ——— because he is tired of commuting to the city."

Responded Day, "I have your letter about your wife's cousin's husband who is a dentist who would like to be a postmaster. You left out a very important piece of information. Does he do extraction work? Because pull helps."

❲ Edward Day, former Postmaster General, tells the story of former Governor Gaylord Nelson of Wisconsin, who was trying out a technique of vote-getting that was actually alien to him. In a small Wisconsin town, Nelson approached a local merchant, a total stranger to him, and said with a big grin and handshake, "I'm Governor Nelson. Haven't I met you some place before?" he said.

"I don't know," said the store owner, "I meet so many people I can't remember them all."

❲ Ex-Postmaster General Edward Day recounts the story of a woman in Kansas who went into her local post office shortly after the 1960 election of John F. Kennedy. When she asked the clerk for fifty cents worth of stamps, he replied, "What denomination?"

"Well, I didn't know it had come to that," retorted the woman angrily. "Baptist."

❲ Former Postmaster General J. Edward Day encountered a particularly puzzling problem in 1963 when a friend sent him an electric hairbrush. Explained Day, "Naturally I was going to send it right back, because that's government policy, to return all gifts."

However, he then noticed that the brush had been damaged. "Obviously it had been busted in the mail," noted Day, "Now I'm torn between two emotions. If I return it, I give away a deficiency of the Post Office Department. If I don't, I violate government policy."

❲ Nominated by the Alfalfa Club as its mock Presidential candidate for 1966, Federal Reserve Chairman William McChesney Martin, Jr., spoofed the "Great Society."

Martin disclosed "a growing feeling of unrest in this land.
. . . The American people are being shackled with second
cars, air-conditioned split levels, and backyard swimming
pools, leaving them dissatisfied and uneasy." He promised
to "restore to the American people an inalienable right—
the right to have something real to worry about. . . . I shall
need only one term in office to achieve a state of affairs in
which no one will be asking what the country can do for
him, but rather what—if anything—can be done for the
country."

⟨ Addressing the 1963 Gridiron Club Dinner, William L.
Beale, Washington Bureau Chief for the Associated Press,
made this backhanded reference to the school-prayer controversy: "In deference to the presence here tonight of the
Chief Justice of the United States, we shall omit the customary invocation."

⟨ Arthur Krock, senior member of the Gridiron Club, was
setting the scene for one of the skits during the Club's 1963
dinner: "The poverty committee of the Chamber of Commerce is meeting. It has a grave problem: how to stay poor
enough so that Washington can make you rich."

⟨ Carl Rowan and Robert Weaver were among the first
Negro guests attending the Gridiron Club's annual dinner
in 1961. Like most of the guests, the two had rented their
white-tie and tails for the occasion. Discussing the evening's events after dinner, Weaver exclaimed to Rowan,
"Lord—isn't this integration expensive?"

❡ In 1966 Chief Justice Earl Warren attended a San Francisco nightspot where a quartet headed by the son of California Attorney General Tom Lynch was appearing. The performance over, Warren turned to Lynch and observed, "Excellent group—much better than my team in Washington. This group sings together all the time. Of course, my group uses a fairly tricky five-four harmony."

❡ One of Secretary of Defense McNamara's favorite theories goes like this: When a man is bald in front it means he is a "thinker"; when he is bald in back, it indicates that he is sexy; and when the baldness in the back merges with the baldness in front, "it's just a man who thinks he's sexy."

❡ John Gardner was extremely optimistic when he took office as Secretary of Health, Education, and Welfare. "We are all faced with a series of great opportunities—brilliantly disguised as insoluble problems."

❡ As Press Secretary for John F. Kennedy, Pierre Salinger apparently shared the President's love for a well-timed quip. Once, needled by newsmen for sticking adamantly to a prepared press release and for avoiding further queries, Salinger explained, "I am not a textual deviate."

❡ When Caroline Kennedy's pet hamsters escaped, White House reporters interrogated the President's Press Secretary Pierre Salinger for additional details. Announced Salinger, "Our security is very tight but these were extremely intelligent hamsters."

⟨["Do you realize," said a slightly wearied Sargent Shriver to a friend in 1964, "that I haven't had a vacation since 1958?"

"What are you talking about?" queried his friend. "You just got back from Palm Beach."

"True," responded Shriver, "but I was with the Kennedys there."

⟨[Sargent Shriver once stated that he was chosen to head the Peace Corps in 1961 because President Kennedy, warned by everyone that the project would be a resounding flop, felt that when the organization's demise came, "it would be easier to fire a relative than a friend."

⟨[Sargent Shriver: "My parents were second cousins. My grandfather and grandmother were also second cousins; and my great-grandfather and great-grandmother were first cousins. That, I should think, is enough to explain all of my peculiarities."

⟨[Late in 1964 Sargent Shriver was asked if he were being groomed for the Vice-Presidency, and he answered, "If a lady says no she means maybe, and if she says maybe, she means yes, and if she says yes, she's no lady!"

⟨[During a commencement address at Kansas State University in 1962, Sargent Shriver had occasion to report that "the [Peace] Corps is working so well that we are the only federal agency that enjoys the combined simultaneous support of Senator Hubert Humphrey and Senator Barry Goldwater."

❨ In 1965, shortly after President Nasser of the United Arab Republic had proclaimed that the United States could go "jump in the salt water," Secretary of State Dean Rusk was sipping a drink at a press reception.

Milton Freidman, correspondent for the Jewish Telegraph Agency, greeted the Secretary of State. "What are you drinking, Mr. Secretary, salt water?"

"No," interposed Undersecretary of State Averell Harriman, "that's water from the Israeli desalinization plant."

❨ During the 1964 Gridiron dinner, newsman Fletcher Knebel proffered this advise to a small African country concerned about not being noticed by Uncle Sam: "The answer is simple. Take his money, burn down his embassy, flirt with the Communists, and then sue him for nonsupport."

❨ Admiral Hyman G. Rickover, outspoken father of atomic power for the Navy, takes a somewhat pessimistic view of certain aspects of the nation's political philosophy. It is Rickover's contention that if the USSR announced that they were going to send a man to Hell, there would be at least two government agencies before the Appropriations Committee of Congress immediately requesting funds to make certain that this country got there first.

❨ Upon leaving his Washington post as Special Presidential Assistant for National Security Affairs to assume the presidency of the Ford Foundation, McGeorge Bundy reminisced about his political career: "I came to Washington as a Republican with the malicious encouragement of two Presidents. I will be a free man next week and I shall register in New York, and, in due course, we'll see how that comes out."

When asked how he would like living in New York City with a salary increase from $30,000 to $75,000, Bundy stated solemnly that it would only mean "being poor on a larger scale."

❨ William J. Brennan, Jr., Associate Justice of the Supreme Court, delivered an address at Marquette University in February, 1965, during which he looked "through the binoculars of history at some sidelights of the court."

"For example, not every appointee to the Court has prized the honor above all else. John Quincy Adams was nominated to the court and confirmed while on a delicate diplomatic mission to Russia. He rejected the appointment out of hand—apparently thinking it either an insult or a devious way of bringing him home—and returned to haggling with the Czar. So you see there is nothing new—from our beginnings, getting tough with Russian dictators has been a good way to get to the White House. . . . It's often said the presence of a particular person or personality at a certain time in history has brought about important judicial reforms. The story of the chancellor who would be a justice is a case in point. He was twice nominated by President Tyler but both times rejected by the Senate. His rejection was puzzling at first because every prominent leader of the New York Bar had strongly endorsed the nomination. But the reason at length came to light. One of the prominent New York lawyers wrote his Senator urging the confirmation. He told the Senator that all of the New York Bar 'are anxious to get rid of a querulous, disagreeable, unpopular chancellor.' Though the man was mild enough in private, on the bench he was highly unconventional and frequently harassed counsel with pointed interrogation and biting sarcasm. Having failed to elevate him out of the state, the New York Bar resorted in desperation to a more drastic remedy. They induced the New York Legislature to abolish the position of chancellor, thus, you see, achieving a notable judicial reform for quite unjudicial purposes.

"Of course, you know, I'm sure, that there have been justices who found other pastures greener after taking their seats. The first Chief Justice, John Jay, was absent in Great Britain as Washington's Special Envoy when he was elected Governor of New York. This opportunity so pleased him that upon his return he promptly resigned as Chief Justice. His colleague, Associate Justice Rutledge, had quit earlier for what seemed to him the more desirable post of Chief Justice of South Carolina. Rutledge was given a recess appointment as Jay's successor as Chief Justice of the United States but, when the Senate convened, it rejected his nomination within minutes after its submission. From that episode arises a conundrum: Is Earl Warren the thirteenth or the fourteenth Chief Justice? I have heard it said that Chief Justice Vinson believed that Rutledge was not in the line of Chief Justices and that he, Vinson, was therefore the twelfth Chief Justice. The present Chief Justice believes that Rutledge was in the line of Chief Justices. At the John Marshall celebration at William and Mary a few years ago, held after the decision in *Brown v. Board of Education,* Chief Justice Warren was the speaker and Virginia's state officials stayed away almost to a man. The program for that event lists thirteen, not fourteen, Chief Justices. Chief Justice Warren has wondered whether this was because William and Mary doesn't recognize Rutledge's claim or because they don't recognize his. Or perhaps, like the hotel that has no thirteenth floor, there has just never been a thirteenth Chief Justice.

"There was a time when people used to refer to 'the color line of the court'—though I hasten to say the reference had nothing to do with segregation. The mention was of the time when Justices Gray, Brown, and White sat in a row. These three Justices were long retired when that expression gave rise to an atrocious pun. At a dinner party attended by Chief Justice Hughes, mention was made of the color line and that those who had made it up no longer sat on the court. This provoked from some wag the awful pun, 'Of course not, the court is all Hughes now.' . . .

"Even the best of criticism—which is often the best precisely because it is the most telling and the most pungent—sometimes disturbs me. But if I need solace when that happens, I can always go back and read that delightfully extravagant sentence in the letter to the editor of *Look* magazine. 'Justice Brennan appears to be the only American in high government with whom I cannot find one iota of fault.' "

❲ Carl Rowan, the Negro former Federal Information Agency head, moved with his wife and children to Washington in 1961, having purchased a home with a large front lawn in a newly integrated neighborhood. One Saturday when Rowan, dressed in Bermuda shorts and a T-shirt, was out mowing the lawn, a white man pulled his car over to the curb and shouted, "Hey, boy, how much do you get for cutting the grass?"

Rowan stopped the power mower, strode over to the car window and smiled, "The lady of the house lets me live with her."

❲ After resigning as Ambassador to Finland to become Director of the United States Intelligence Agency, Carl Rowan received a letter from a distant cousin. It read, "Only in America could a humble boy from Middle Tennessee rise to such an important position in the Government. Could you spare $300?"

Rowan replied. "Thanks for your good wishes. Only in America could one leave a position as head of an embassy with 120 employees to direct an agency with 12,120 employees—and take a cut in pay. Could *you* spare $300?"

❨ E. William Henry, Chairman of the Federal Communications Commission, received a communication opposing an FCC proposal to increase its fees for processing broadcast applications and was moved to the point of verse. His reply:

> The broadcast goose, well-stuffed and sleek
> Can ill afford to mourn
> If we, the FCC, now seek
> One kernel of its corn.
> In lands where private grain is banned
> A goose so plump and fatty
> Would have its liver ground and canned
> For governmental pâté,
> But no feather will we harm
> No golden goose-fruit beg;
> Fie on this flap of mild alarm
> It's simply laid an egg.

❨ As guest of honor at a luncheon in 1965, FCC Chairman E. William Henry was introduced as a real celebrity —an official who had been featured in an article in *Playboy* magazine. Noted Henry, "Being in *Playboy* didn't worry me. The article was on page 117. What worried me was that it took me forty-five minutes to get to it."

❨ Former Supreme Court Justice Fred Vinson tells this tale:

"It seems there were five horses entered in a horse race. Four were quoted at normal odds but the fifth horse, Speed Demon, was a long 30 to 1. A mild little man went up to the bookie and bet $500 on Speed Demon. The bookie took the bet and reduced the odds to 20 to 1.

"Pretty soon the little man came back and bet another $500 at 20 to 1 on Speed Demon. This time the bookie marked Speed Demon down to 15 to 1. Again and again the little man came back with $500 bets while the odds sank to 10, to 5, to 2 to 1, and finally to even money. At this point, even the hardhearted bookie relented. 'Mister,' he pleaded, 'don't bet any more money on that horse. You're throwing your money away. Speed Demon can't win.'

" 'How do you know?' asked the man. 'Because I own Speed Demon!' exclaimed the bookie in exasperation. The little man whistled softly. 'Brother, it's going to be a slow race,' he replied. 'I own the other four.' "

⟨ During his 1964 lecture tour of India as Supreme Court Justice, Arthur Goldberg was frequently addressed at one reception as "Justice Goldwater."

"That's OK," he remarked, "I have tremendous respect for Senator Goldberg."

⟨ Arthur J. Goldberg, United States Ambassador to the United Nations, relates the story of an Iowa judge who was once called to San Francisco as a substitute for an ailing colleague. One of the first cases he was called upon to decide involved admiralty law. Being from Iowa, he had no specialized knowledge in admiralty law, so he asked the litigants if they wouldn't prefer that the case be postponed until the regular judge returned. The litigants said no, they would rather have him decide it. Upon which the Iowa judge rejoined, "All right. But I want to make one thing clear. Let there be no moaning at the bar when I put out to sea."

◖ Supreme Court Justice Tom C. Clark recalls that as Attorney General one of the important cases he litigated was one that resulted in the largest contempt fine ever assessed in a federal court. The case involved the strike of the United Mine Workers and the sentence was against it and its president, John L. Lewis, for violation of an injunction. Says Clark, "The 'wags' called it the 'Lewis and Clark disposition.' "

"Several months later," recalls the justice, "I was called upon to introduce President Truman in my hometown of Dallas. The traditional introduction was, of course, 'I give you the President of the United States.' But in my exhuberance, my introduction was, 'My fellow Dallasites, I am proud to introduce my best client—the only person who ever knocked out Joe Lewis—the President of the United States.' I have never heard the end of this mix-up of 'Joe' for 'John L.' "

◖ Fred Korth, former Secretary of the Navy once received a series of heat treatments in the Pentagon dispensary for a minor pain in the back of his neck. About the fourth day, when he presented himself for the daily application, the attendant said, "Mr. Secretary, Bethesda Naval Hospital says to put you in traction this morning. Let's get rid of your trouble once and for all."

"He had me stretch out on the table, while he fastened my legs with straps, clapped a leather harness around my neck, and proceeded to stretch the noose tighter for a full half hour.

"When I returned to my office after this somewhat painful experience, one of the Assistant Secretaries of the Navy dropped by to tell me that he was on his way to the therapeutic room—he was going to get his neck stretched and would return in about thirty minutes.

Recalls Korth, "I then realized that the treatment had already been given that morning—to the wrong man!"

❲ The following letter presented an extremely interesting problem to former Attorney General William P. Rogers. It was referred to him by President Eisenhower for his legal opinion.

Dear Mr. President:

I would like to know if the law makes school teachers get drafted in the service. If they do, I know one who has not been. His name is ——— and he is 26 years old.

Thank you.

(Signed by a ten-year-old boy in Pennsylvania)

❲ The following plan for relieving poverty in Appalachia was offered to former Postmaster General John Gronouski by a sixteen-year-old boy: "His idea was both simple and ingenious. He wanted us to print a few thousand stamps with deliberate errors in them, which would make them quite valuable. These stamps we were to send to the towns in Appalachia where people would buy them for five cents apiece, then resell them to stamp collectors for $1,000 or $10,000 or whatever the market could stand. And this would cure poverty."

❴ Every year some of America's finest and funniest political satire is unveiled at the newspapermen's Gridiron Club
dinner. At the 1965 affair, three newsmen impersonating
unsuccessful Republican candidates for the 1964 Presidential nomination sang this devastating little ditty to the tune
of "With a Little Bit of Luck":

SCRANTON:

> The Lord above gave Scranton an
>   adviser—
> A man the voters really, truly like.
> The Lord above gave Scranton an
>   adviser
> But—with a little bit of luck,
> With a little bit of luck,
> In the next campaign it won't be
>   Ike.

ROMNEY:

> The Lord above said "Romney,
>   choose a party."
> But didn't say for which team I
>   should bat.
>
> And so I chose to choose the Grand Old Party.
> But—with a little bit of luck,
> With a little bit of luck,
> They'll mistake me for a Democrat.

ROCKEFELLER:

> The Gallup Poll gave me my inspiration.
> Lou Harris put no limit on my goals.
> And Roper said I'd win the nomination.
> But—with the Rockefeller luck,
> With the Rockefeller luck,

Hardly anyone believed those polls.
With a little bit, with a little bit,
With a little bit of luck they'd
doubt the polls.

ALL:

Oh, we can walk the straight and narrow,
And with a little bit of luck we won't get stuck.
The GOP last year was made for Barry,
To share his views, although his goose was cooked,
The GOP had more than it could carry,
But—with a little bit of luck,
With a little bit of luck,
Not a single one of us got hooked.

❨ The Air Force Academy cadets received this telegram from former Air Force Secretary Eugene Zuckert on the eve of their big game with Army: "It is important to keep in mind that the purpose of the Air Force Academy is to turn out career officers, not varsity athletes. While football has a place at the Academy, it should not be a dominant interest.
"Accordingly, I issue the following orders: Beat Army!"

❨ Alice Roosevelt Longworth, daughter of President Theodore Roosevelt and widow of House Speaker Nicholas Longworth, is famed as one of the most penetrating of the Washington wits. She says of herself, "Anyone who has been around as long as I have has many recollections—but I'm still able to shrug the shoulders and lift the eyebrows. I might possibly be a footnote a hundred years from now."
Mrs. Longworth states that she has "no use for self-pity or for people who take defeat seriously. All those people

who sob and moan . . . people that whine and snarl. That's a nice thing about Barry Goldwater. He never indulged in wincing or whining.

"I knew Goldwater only slightly, but every time we would run into each other, we were apt to murmur, 'Bucky O'Neill! Bucky O'Neill!' He was the first Rough Rider killed in the Spanish-American War in Cuba, and he is a hero of Arizona. That was about the extent of our conversations. Then in 1963, I was invited to a birthday party in honor of Eisenhower here in Washington. I didn't know my plans until the day before, when I called to see if there was still room for me. The committee lady seemed pleased and said she would find a very good place for me at the dinner. I arrived and found myself seated on the side next to Barry Goldwater, and on the other side was some negligible politician. Bill Miller, then chairman of the Republican National Committee, made the main speech. He assured us that when the Eisenhowers were in the White House no one did the twist in the historic East Room and no one had been thrown into a pool fully clad. I thought to myself: this is where I came in. I told Goldwater of the criticism of my father's use of the East Room for far more violent and vigorous activities, such as judo and singlestick. And regarding the comment on people going into pools with their clothes on, I mentioned that in 1905 I was on a steamer going across the Pacific; a canvas tank was rigged up on the deck. One day I appeared in a linen coat and skirt, and some friend dared me to go in like that. I said, 'Let me take off my shoes,' and I dived in. I told Goldwater all this. Perhaps he didn't hear what I said. His only response was a murmur."

Discussing Theodore and Franklin Roosevelt, Mrs. Longworth noted, "My father died in 1919, so there never was any conflict between them, because Franklin hadn't emerged. He very possibly wouldn't have emerged if my father hadn't emerged, and my father might not have emerged if Czolgosz hadn't killed McKinley. Who can tell?

"Were it not for Czolgosz, we'd all be back in our brownstone-front houses. That's where we'd be. And I would have married for money and been divorced for a good cause."

❰ Mrs. Alice Roosevelt Longworth tells the story of the merchant seaman who was being interrogated under the provisions of the McCarran Act. The investigator queried, "Do you have any pornographic literature?"

"Pornographic literature!" exclaimed the seaman indignantly. "I don't even have a pornograph!"

❰ Alice Roosevelt Longworth, daughter of Teddy Roosevelt, was delighted with Lyndon Johnson's breaking of a sartorial precedent when he wore a dark business suit to his inauguration in 1964. Stated Mrs. Longworth, "I think he ought to put on one of those string ties and a Stetson and high-heeled boots."

6. Favorite Stories from Capitol Hill

⟨ THE FOLLOWING is a selection of the most beloved tales, yarns, anecdotes, and such, as told by our nation's legislators. Many of them have been put to good use in "warming up" an audience, or by making a telling point by way of analogy. But, just as often, these wonderful tales are recounted out of a simple love of humorous storytelling that seems to be as natural a part of American politics as the two-party system itself.

⟨ A banker went to his doctor for a physical checkup. After thorough tests the doctor's verdict came: "You're as sound as a dollar."

"Holy smoke!" exclaimed the banker. "As bad as that!"

And fainted dead away.

Representative Joe Kilgore of Texas

223

❲ The rules of the procedure of the Houses of Congress are complicated, and woe betide the young man who doesn't know them. Even before Congress convened I had started to read the rules and was very much interested in them. Of course, when Congress actually convened I wanted to be there and learn more about the rules in practice. I remember on the second day of this Congress—really the first legislative, business day, because the first day was merely the swearing in—there were a great number of Congressmen standing in the front, or the well, of the House. I was sitting in the back and all I could hear was the other members say, "Mumble, mumble, mumble," and then the Speaker would say, "Without objection, so ordered."

Being of an inquisitive mind, I went down one of the side aisles, so that I could listen more carefully to what the mumbo-jumbo was that these Congressmen were saying, because I felt that someday I would be down there too, asking for whatever it was they were asking for.

One of my colleagues, a freshman Congressman from Connecticut, was also interested so he went down too. Only, unfortunately, he went down one of the main aisles of the House, and was standing there listening to what was being requested by the other Congressmen.

Suddenly the Speaker of the House turned and said, "The Chair recognizes the gentleman from Connecticut!"

My friend from Connecticut looked to his left, there was no one there from Connecticut, he looked to his right, there was no one there from Connecticut.

On the second day of his tenure as a Congressman, he had the floor of the house, and nothing to say! All he could do was utter a "No, No, No, NO!" and sink feebly into the nearest seat. He was roundly applauded for having given the shortest speech in the record of the House of Representatives.

Representative William S. Moorhead of Pennsylvania

⟨ The following is a copy of an actual letter I received from one of my constituents shortly after my election. I had made a campaign promise to get every letter answered within forty-eight hours of the time it was received—I answered the letter within forty-eight hours, but didn't get her husband back in that time!

Honorable Gale Schisler
Member of Congress
Washington, D. C.

Dear Congressman Schisler:

I would like to be the first one to write you. You know, they say when things don't go right to write your Congressman.

Well, things aren't going right. I live in a small community of about 600 people. You know, where everybody knows everybody else. My problem is this: My husband is gone, and since he's gone the toilet is overflowing . . . the lights have been turned off for not paying the bill . . . the telephone is out of order . . . the dog is expecting pups . . . the washing machine is leaking . . . my neighbors' kids' noses are running all the time . . . and my own kids are driving me nuts.

Can you help me? Maybe you could pass a bill in Congress helping us poor neglected housewives.

Sincerely,
Mrs. D. G.

Representative Gale Schisler of Illinois

⟨ A certain English professor, having been out late the night before "doing the town," devised a clever scheme to avoid delivering his usual one-hour lecture, the last thing he felt like doing, to his eight o'clock class the next morning. He would ask them to write a theme containing such difficult and incongruous subject matter that it would be impossible for them to finish before the hour was up.

He addressed the class as follows:

"Good morning, class. Today we will write a theme containing all of the following subjects—religion, royalty, sex, and mystery."

Just as he had settled back in his chair, a student from the back of the room came forward with his completed theme. It read, "Oh, Lord! The Princess is pregnant! Who done it?"

Representative Peter A. Garland of Maine

❲ Like most clubs of its type, my Rotary Club in Lamar, Colorado, has a membership restricted to one of each economic category, such as one hardware salesman, one printer, one doctor, one dentist, and so on.

A young Methodist minister moved into town with a very delightful family. We had him as guest at our Rotary Club a number of times and wanted to take him into the club. But, there was one problem—we already had a Protestant minister in the club. However, in typical fashion of small-town neighbors, we found a way to get around this and invited him one day to join the club.

The president told him at the meeting that we were delighted with him and that he and his family fitted into the community beautifully, that they were great assets, that we would be proud to have him as a member of our club. The president added that there was only one hitch, that as he knew we have this system of categorizing our members and that the category for Protestant minister was filled, there was only one other category that was vacant at the time, and that if he did not mind we would bring him in as a hog caller. The minister stood up and thanked the president and told him that he was delighted with this honor, that he felt it was particularly significant that they would accept him as one of their own in the town and then added quietly, "I came here as a shepherd of men, but of course you know your people better than I."

Senator Gordon Allott of Colorado

❐ Politics does indeed make strange bedfellows. Sometimes one can find himself making common cause with people of whom he is generally far from approving. It brings to mind the story about the teacher who asked how many of her students wanted to go to Heaven. All except Willie raised their hands.

"Why, don't you want to go, Willie?" she exclaimed.

"Yes," was the response, "but not with this bunch."

Senator Frank Church of Idaho

❐ A Midwestern Congressman was campaigning in the rural area of his district. Approaching a farmer at work in his field, the Congressman stated his name, made a short political speech, and wound up with an impassioned plea for the farmer's vote. Apparently hard of hearing, the farmer failed to comprehend. After several frustrating attempts, the shouting Congressman finally got his message through. "Oh, you'll get my vote, son," drawled the farmer. "Anyone would be better than that feller who's in there now!"

Representative David S. King of Utah

❐ My favorite story pertains to one of my experiences in doorbell ringing.

As I approached an average-sized house, I noticed a

small boy on a tricycle in front of the steps leading to the front porch. I inquired of the small boy whether his mother was at home and he replied, "Yes, she is." I then knocked on the door but received no answer. After waiting a minute or so, I knocked again, but again received no answer. As I turned to leave the porch I looked down at the boy and said to him, "I thought you told me your mother was at home?" The boy replied, "She *is* at home, but we don't live here."

Representative James Harvey of Michigan

⟮ One time a Quaker from up North moved down South to try his hand at mule farming. He had never plowed with a mule before and did not know how stubborn a mule could be. He hitched the mule to the plow, and said "Gid-e-up." The old mule didn't budge. This went on for several minutes while the Quaker got madder and madder. Finally, he walked around, got in front of the mule, caught the bridle, looked the mule straight in the eye and said, "Old mule, thou knowest that I cannot strike thee. Thou knowest because of my religion that I cannot even curse thee. But what thou knowest not is that I can sell thee to a Baptist Deacon who will beat—— out of thee!"

Representative G. Elliot Hagen of Georgia

⟮ Asked how he came out in a family quarrel, the man said: "Aw, she came crawling to me on her knees." Then he added: "She kept yelling, 'Come out from under that bed, you coward!' "

Representative Craig Hosmer of California

⟮ After being in the Congress for a few years, I had begun to feel that I had acquired some acquaintance among my constituents. Then during one of my campaigns, while driving through my district, I picked up a farmer who wanted a ride to the county seat town. He inquired about my identity and I told him I was a candidate for reelection to the Congress.

"Oh, yes, I know you," he said, "you're Albert Gore."

To which I replied, "No, I'm not Albert Gore although we are neighbors and good friends."

"Why surely," he exclaimed, "I should have known right off, you're Senator Ross Bass."

I tried now to be more direct and said: "No, I'm Edgar Evins' son," indicating my hometown.

"To be sure, you're the fellow who raises Tennessee Walking Horses."

Again I had to indicate that he was mistaking my identity, as he was referring to my brother. At this, my friend began to smile and complete recognition.

"Of course," he said, "I have you straight now—you're Judge Smartt's son-in-law."

This, with a newly found humility, I now had to confess, was true.

Representative Joe L. Evins of Tennessee

❨ A young man who had always been very active in church work and who had always been a dutiful son to his father, who was suffering from a very advanced case of deafness, arrived home from church in the company of a stranger.

"Dad," he said, "I would like for you to meet the new deacon."

"What's that you say, did you say New Dealer?"

"No, Dad, the new deacon. He is the son of a bishop."

"They all are son, they all are!"

Representative Thomas N. Downing of Virginia

《 One of the stories that always made a hit with me concerns a state senator who found that a bill introduced by himself was on the calendar for final passage with nothing of its original intent left except his name and the bill number.

In explaining his vote against his own bill, he said, "I find myself reminded of the ancient story of the dove that left in the morning and returned in the evening, a raven."

Representative John H. Dent of Pennsylvania

《 A politician running scared for reelection approached a recipient of many past political favors.

"Well, Joe, who are you going to vote for this time? For me again, aren't you?"

Joe hesitated and then allowed as how he hadn't made up his mind.

"What do you mean, you don't know, after all the things I have done for you," the politician said. "I got you a job once when you needed it; took care of speeding tickets for that son of yours; gave your uncle a job in the city dump; saw that your brother-in-law got on relief. What does a guy have to do?"

"Yeah, maybe you did those things," Joe acknowledged. "But what have you done for me lately?"

Senator Claiborne Pell of Rhode Island

《 A lovely parish in my district decided that its good padre had worked long and hard and the parishioners should express their appreciation in a tangible way by raising the money for him to take a vacation.

The padre decided on an ocean voyage as it would afford time for quiet repose, as well as an opportunity to catch up on his reading, which he had neglected because of arduous parish duties.

The first day at sea was beautiful and sunny, and the good father took a favorite text and flopped into a deck chair to enjoy the sun and good literature.

In about ten minutes, a young man came along and sat in the chair beside him. Noticing that he was a man of the cloth, he said conversationally, "I'm an atheist." The good padre pretended not to hear.

A few minutes later, the young man tried again. "I'm an atheist," he repeated, in a loud voice. Again, the padre paid no attention.

Exasperated, the unwelcome intruder stood up and fairly shouted, "I'm an atheist—aren't you interested in saving my soul?"

With that, the long-suffering padre closed his book, glowered at the young man, and said disgustedly, "Couldn't you go to hell quietly?"

Representative Carroll D. Kearns of Pennsylvania

◖ When I was a young prosecuting attorney, a lady appeared in my office every weekend, all bruised and battered and beaten by her drunken husband. We always filed an affidavit, and on Monday morning we went to police court and when she was placed on the stand she always claimed that her husband had not molested her.

I remember one time she had a very black eye. I said, "Mrs. H., how did you get that black eye?" She said, "Oh, that is where I bumped into the door." She was back the next weekend and, again, we filed an affidavit. When we appeared in court Monday morning I said to her, "Mrs. H., how did you get that scar on your forehead?" She replied, "Oh, that is where I fell over a chair." The next weekend, we filed another affidavit and in court I asked her how she got the scar on her arm. She said, "Oh, that is just where I ran into the stove." The charges were, of course, dismissed.

Then, the next weekend she appeared in my office and wanted to file charges. I refused to file them for her. I said, "Mrs. H., there isn't any use, you will just go down to court on Monday and say your husband didn't molest you and the charges will be dismissed." She said, "Just look at this black eye." I said, "Oh, that's just where you bumped into the door." She said, "But look at this scar on my arm." I said, "But that's just where you ran into the stove." Then she said, "Look at this scar on my leg." I said, "Oh, that's just where you fell over a chair." She then said, bewildered, "Well, what am I going to do?" I said, "Why don't you just take matters into your own hands and hit him over the head with the poker." She said, "He's much bigger than I am and I couldn't do that." I said, "Well, wait until he's asleep and then beat him up."

I was called to the police station in the middle of the night with the announcement that Mrs. H. had killed her husband. I said, "Well, I am sure that it was in self-defense." The chief of police said, "No, she beat him over the head while he was asleep and was, in fact, beating him when the police arrived on the scene." I said, "Good Lord, what am I going to do now?" I went back to her cell and as I entered she screamed, "Just look what you've done to me now. I wait till he goes to sleep like you said and hit him over the head with the poker like you said and here I am in a police cell." Fortunately, Mr. H. did not die.

I didn't see Mrs. H. again for a long time. One day we met on Main Street and I said, "How is your husband doing?" She said, "Oh, he is the finest man you ever saw." I said, "Well, does he ever get drunk any more and beat you?" She hesitated a moment and then said, "Well, when he does, all I say is, 'You hide the poker!'"

Representative Winfield K. Denton of Indiana

It is easy enough to smile
With a girl, a glass, and a song
But the man worthwhile
Is the man who can smile
When he has brought his old woman along.

Senator Karl E. Mundt of South Dakota

❨ Two friends were playing golf when one of the men had a heart attack. Though they were at the farthest green from the clubhouse, his friend managed to carry the stricken man back.

"I doubt if I could have pulled him through if you hadn't carried him here," the doctor said after treating the patient. "That was really heroic. Why, he weighs at least 250 pounds, and I think you'd better let me take a look at you."

The golfer assured the doctor that, though he was tired, he was quite all right.

"Nonsense," the doctor said. "Carrying 250 pounds that far is quite a strain."

"Nothing to that, doc," the man said. "What was exhausting was putting him down and picking him up again between shots."

Representative Harlan Hagen of California

❨ An East Texas sharecropper family was asleep one night on a pallet in their one-room shack when the ol' houn' dog commenced to howl outdoors, and it woke up Papa.

Papa turned over and punched Mama and said, "Mama, go on out and see what's wrong with the ol' houn' dog. I would go m'self, but I'm jus' too tahrd to move."

Mama rolled over and punched Son and said, "Son,

would you go out there and see what's wrong with that dog. I would go m'self, but I'm jus' too tahrd to move."

Son turned over and said to Sister, "Sis, go on out and see what's wrong with the ol' houn' dog. I would go m'self, but I'm jus' too tahrd to move."

Sister turned over to little Bud and said, "Little Bud, go on out and see what's wrong with that ol' hound' dog. I would go m'self, but I'm jus' too tahrd to move."

So Little Bud turned over and there wasn't nobody else there so he went on out to see what was wrong with the ol' houn' dog.

When he come back in the house, Papa said, "Son, what was wrong with the ol' houn' dog, anyway?"

And Little Bud said:

"Well, he was a settin' on a cockleburr and he's jus' too tahrd to move."

Senator John G. Tower of Texas

❲ All of you remember the story of early American history when George Washington was growing up on his daddy's ranch in the High Plains of West Texas. Well, on that ranch there was a beautiful mesquite tree. George's daddy loved that tree. Not only because it was a beautiful mesquite tree, but also because it was the only tree for fifty miles in any direction.

One day, when his daddy was out on the range rounding up a few mavericks and strays, George pulled on his boots, picked up his Bowie knife and went out and whittled down that mesquite tree. When his daddy got home, he took little George out behind the corral and asked him, "George, who whittled down my mesquite tree?"

"I did it, Daddy," said George. "I cannot tell a lie."

"Pack your things, son," his daddy said. "We're moving to Virginia. You'll never get along like that in Texas."

Senator John G. Tower of Texas

◖ When I first became a member of Congress in 1945, I had, and still have, an abundance of pride in my native state. I immediately began telling my colleagues in the Congress that West Virginia is God's country. The loud-mouthed braggart delegation from Texas and the stuffed-shirt delegation from Virginia wanted to argue the point. My reply was to tell them about a man who died sometime ago, and for some unbelievable reason he found himself in Heaven. He started to look the place over and was sur-prised at the beauty, grandeur of everything. He was enjoy-ing himself, and one day while taking a walk down a quiet lane, he glanced to the left and there he saw a group of ten or twelve men with balls and chains on their ankles. He immediately began to worry about the existence of this kind of situation in Heaven, in the face of all the other splendors. His curiosity got the best of him, and he began to ask questions. No one would tell him anything, and one day he happened to come across Saint Peter. He asked Saint Peter for an explanation, and Saint Peter laid his hands on his shoulders and said, "Brother, there is a good explanation for this situation. Those boys are from West Virginia, and if I did not keep them hobbled they would go home for the weekend."

Representative Cleveland M. Bailey of West Virginia

◖ One morning during the war, I got in a taxi in front of the Mayflower Hotel, and a very charming lady asked per-mission to share the cab—as cabs were hard to find at that particular time.

As the taxi pulled away from the hotel, the driver turned on the radio and the news commentator was repeating something I had said the day before on the floor of the Senate.

The very charming lady turned to me and said, "Those

Senators make me tired—they don't know what they are talking about and yet they are always shooting their mouths off. We would be better off without them."

I agreed with her, never disclosing, of course, my identity.

(Late) Senator Homer Capehart of Indiana

❨ In October, 1961, President Kennedy flew to Oklahoma to dedicate a highway in Ouachita National Forest. It was an informal ceremony at which I presided.

Near the end of the program, I asked the President if he would sign his name on the lectern as a memento of the occasion. The President took out his pen and came up to the lectern.

"Mr. President," I said, "this reminds me of an incident that happened to another President—Harry Truman." And while President Kennedy signed his name, I told the story:

"President Truman was stumping the country on a campaign train. When he started to get into his bed one night, he noticed a small black object on the clean white sheet. He summoned the porter.

" 'What is that on the sheet?' asked the President.

" 'Now, Mr. President,' grinned the porter, 'you know that's a bedbug.'

'Well,' snorted Truman, 'I didn't know this great railroad had any bedbugs.'

" 'Oh, it's not ours, Mr. President,' retorted the porter. 'If it was, it would have Pullman on it!' "

(Late) Senator Robert Kerr of Oklahoma

❨ As the Republican nominee for Congress in a special election in 1960, I was virtually unknown outside my home county. The name "Schneebeli" presented quite a problem, particularly after my two immediate predecessors who were Al Bush and Bob Rich.

Several leading political figures came into the area to assist in my campaign. At one town, after inspirational speeches by three of the visiting political personages, the county chairman arose to introduce me with high praises. Having difficulty with my name, he kept prolonging the introduction, hoping that he could recall it to mind. Finally, he gave up and, leaning over to his neighbor he said, "What's the name of this guy running for Congress?" The loudspeaker, of course, was wide open, and the crowd heard the urgent and excited whisper. At least the group was relaxed by the time I got up to add my few words!

Representative Herman T. Schneebeli of Pennsylvania

⟨ A woman with a small child was traveling on the train. A man across the aisle kept staring at them. She finally asked him why he was staring, and he replied that her baby was just about the ugliest child he had ever seen. She became so incensed that she got up to report this outrage to the conductor.

When she found him and complained about the treatment she had received, the conductor said, "Now, I know you are upset, but this is a public conveyance and I can't put the man off the train. Why don't you come back to the dining car and I'll get you a cup of coffee to soothe your nerves. And while we are there, I'll get your monkey a nice banana."

Representative Laurence J. Burton of Utah

⟨ My opponent for office, in what I considered a moment of rash enthusiasm, said, "In a few months the Democratic candidate's wife will be sleeping in the White House." I responded as follows: "Your statement reminds me of the story about the campaign between McKinley and William Jennings Bryan, which took place at the turn of the century. One cold night William Jennings Bryan, the silver-tongued orator from the West, whose famous Cross of Gold speech brought him international renown, told an audience of 200 shivering people that 'tonight my beloved wife sleeps in a humble inn two miles from here but comes next January she will be sleeping in the White House.' At that time, an oaf in the audience shouted out boldly, 'Well, if she is, she will be sleeping with McKinley because he is going to be the occupant of the White House!' "

Representative Edwin B. Dooley of New York

❡ Two banquets were being held at the Shoreham Hotel in Washington, D.C. One banquet was attended by members of the Distillers' Union and the other by a group from the Women's Christian Temperance Union. Everything went well until the serving of dessert. At this point the desserts for the two groups were accidentally switched, and the WCTU people were served the "spiked" watermelon intended for the distillers.

The headwaiter decided against making a point of the accident. He said nothing until the women were finishing their dessert. Then he stepped over to one of the waiters and asked whether the women had commented on the watermelon.

To which the waiter replied, "I didn't hear any comments from the ladies on the melon, but I did notice that all of them were putting the seeds in their pocketbooks."

Representative D. R. Matthews of Florida

❲ I am quite short in physical stature, only five feet four inches tall. I was speaking at a rural school in my district and was giving the audience everything I had. At the conclusion of my speech, a little boy came up to me and said, "Mister, you sure inspired me today."

I beamed at the lad and pursued the matter a little further. I asked him what I had said that had been inspiring, thinking that whatever it was, I could use it on another audience.

"It wasn't anything you said," replied the boy. "I just figure if a little squirt like you can be elected to Congress, I can become President of the United States."

Representative Carl Albert of Oklahoma

❲ Once, when President Theodore Roosevelt was addressing a meeting, a man in the back kept shouting, "I am a Democrat!" When he was unable to ignore the interruptions any longer, Roosevelt said, "If the gentleman in the back is so anxious to speak, why doesn't he tell us why he is a Democrat?"

The man stood up and replied, "I am a Democrat because my father was a Democrat and my grandfather was a Democrat." Gleefully, the President then said, "I see. Now if your father had been a jackass and your grandfather had been a jackass, what would that make you?"

Quick as a flash, the man shot back, "A Republican!"

Representative Jonathan B. Bingham of New York

❲ In South Carolina any candidate for office is likely to be linked for political purposes or otherwise with some other candidate running for another office. In order to avoid being linked with another candidate in the public eye and becoming involved in his race, I frequently tell the story that I now relate.

Two old maid sisters lived in a small Southern town and each owned a very fine female cat. They never let the cats out of the house to mingle with the common variety. Time passed and one of the old maids caught a beau and was married. As she left for her honeymoon, her sister made her promise to wire from New York. The newly married sister was true to her word and wired her old maid sister:

"I don't care what you do with your cat, but let my cat out."

Representative Robert W. Hemphill of South Carolina

(Two judges who were far from being the best of friends were arrested for speeding. By coincidence, they were ordered to appear in court on the same day. On arriving at the courtroom they found the chambers empty, so they decided to appear before each other and thus dispose of the speeding charges.

The first judge donned his legal attire, mounted the bench, rapped with his gavel, "First case," he intoned.

"You are charged with exceeding the speed limit," he said sternly to the other judge, "How do you plead?"

"Guilty, your honor," answered the other judge.

"You are hereby fined five dollars by this court. Step down. Next case."

Then they changed places, the second judge mounting the bench, and the first promptly pleaded guilty.

"Well," said the judge now sitting on the bench, "this is the second case of this kind we've had this morning. They're becoming far too numerous. Twenty dollars or ten days in jail."

Representative George F. Senner, Jr., of Arizona

❲ I once knew a man who was addicted to playing the horses and who always lost. One day at the racetrack, after once again losing heavily, he saw a priest give the holy blessing to a horse in one of the stalls at the starting gate. Much to his surprise, this horse came in first. At the start of the next race, he saw the same priest giving the blessing to another horse, just as before. Sure enough, this horse also won.

Before the next race, he saw the priest give the blessing to another horse. On seeing this, he ran to the betting window to place all the money he had left on the horse that the priest had just blessed. He thought to himself that finally, after all these years, he'd bet on a winner.

The bell rang for the next race and the horses charged out of the gate and down the track, with his horse far behind. By the time the rest of the horses were making the last turn and heading down the home stretch, his horse was a quarter of a mile behind and slowing down with every stride. Finally, the horse came to a complete stop, rolled over, and died right on the track.

Needless to say, the forlorn racing fan was perplexed. He ran and found the priest. "Father," he asked, "what happened to the last horse you blessed? The two other horses you blessed finished first, but the last horse rolled over and died right on the track."

"That's the trouble with you non-Catholics," lamented the priest. "You can't tell the difference between the holy blessing and the last rites!"

Representative Clement J. Zablocki of Wisconsin

❲ A preacher down in Mississippi had led a rather checkered life before he selected the ministry as a vocation. He then moved to a distant part of the state where he became pastor of a church in a small town. One Sunday morning, as he rose in the pulpit to address his congregation, his roving eyes caught sight of one of his former friends, a cellmate with whom he had done time before engaging in ministerial work.

Being a resourceful person, the preacher soon overcame his embarrassment. With his eyes firmly fixed on his old friend, he made this announcement:

"Brethren and Sistren: This morning I had selected for my text the Ten Commandments. However, as I size up my audience, I think I will change my text to the following: 'And I say unto them as sees me and thinks they recognize me, sayest thou nothing and I'll see that thou receivest thy reward hereafter.' "

Representative William M. Colmer of Mississippi

❴ New York City counterfeiters were turning out bogus money. Due to some mechanical defect a batch of bills came off the press in eighteen-dollar denominations. The counterfeiters were about to destroy the bills when a fellow "city slicker" advised that he could take them to the hills of West Virginia, where the people, he said, "wouldn't know the difference." So he took off for the hills.

At a country store in the mountains, the city fellow threw one of the eighteen-dollar bills on the counter and said, "Hi, Sport, how about a little change?"

"Sure," the proprietor drawled, without blinking an eye, "how would you like it—two nines or three sixes?"

Senator Jennings Randolph of West Virginia

❴ The Trotter brothers had a contract to carry the mail between Huttonville in Randolph County and Staunton, Virginia. In the winter of 1855, after a trip south, heavy snowfall prevented their return across the mountain. The people of Tygarts River Valley, irritated by the delay in their mail, complained to authorities in Washington. The Post Office Department relayed the complaint to the Trotters, who replied as follows:

Staunton, Virginia
1855

Mr. Postmaster General
Washington, D. C.

Sirs:

If you knock the gable end out of Hell and back it up against Cheat Mountain and rain fire and brimstone for 40 days and 40 nights, it won't melt the snow enough to get your damned mail through on time.

Yours truly,

TROTTER BROTHERS

by James Trotter

Senator Jennings Randolph of West Virginia

⟨ "You and I as holders of public office have had much experience with lobbyists and all sorts of special-interest organizations. Lately I have been of the opinion that there must be a 'Primer for Pitiless Pressure Groups' because nothing else would explain why some of those Lobbyists act as they do. Let me suggest what might be in this 'Primer,' which could have the subtitle 'The Art and Practice of Strongarm Legislation':

"1. Be sure of your timing. Catch your public official when he is extremely busy and fully occupied. His resistance will be low and you can knock his guard down. Of course, he will hate you and swear vengeance on your cause, but you will have made quite an impression.

"2. Always stress the number of voters you 'represent' —upping the actual number about ten or a hundred times. And don't be subtle about what the voters will do to 'politicians' who don't vote as you tell them. Your ability to frighten an official is limited only by your opposition's ability to frighten him in the other direction.

"3. Don't hesitate to embarrass an officeholder. Nail him as he is talking with his friends or confront him with a menacing crowd of your cohorts. This will keep him off base, which is why this tactic is referred to as a 'base method.'

"4. Whether you are being vague or specific, be emphatic about it. Here's how to be emphatically vague: Speak of 'H. 1378.' Since there is a new H. 1378 and a new S. 4888 in each Congress, the public official will have to look up the current bill and this prevents him from discussing the subject intelligently. Here's how to be emphatically specific: Write him a six-page letter with all the details. Pour on the reasons. Don't believe those people who think one good reason is enough.

"5. Be zealous. See the public official not once but many times. Write to him, wire him, and don't forget to phone him at home around dinnertime. He will be glad to get away from the children for a long chat with you. Sheer numbers count. Besides, a single visit can hardly justify the expense account you will submit to your employers.

"6. Corner your officeholder at a social gathering. Be sure to monopolize his attention. It is helpful to load him with a mass of details about your project while he is trying to eat. He will be sure to remember all of it—and you.

"7. If all of these tactics hurt your cause, get another cause."

Senator Hugh Scott of Pennsylvania

⟪ During a campaign, I spoke repeatedly in every section of my district, in Alabama. Many times I noticed persons in the audience that I was sure had been among previous audiences. This bothered me a little because, having to speak so much, I had to repeat some of my speeches rather frequently.

In Bessemer, Alabama, I spoke to the Kiwanis Club one evening. The next week I spoke to a church men's club at Bessemer and noticed on the front row of my audience a man who had heard the Kiwanis speech. I tried to change a few phrases and add a few thoughts but it was the same basic speech and it disturbed me somewhat that this gentleman was having to listen to it again. Several days later I fulfilled a speaking engagement at the Bessemer Council of Civic, Social, and Religious Forces of the same community, and, much to my chagrin, the same gentleman was again in the front row. I at least wanted to let him know that I was not oblivious to his being present on three different occasions and hearing the same speech. After the meeting I went up to him and offered my apologies for having possibly bored him by delivering the same address three times and was taken aback when he replied: "Oh, don't feel bad, Congressman. Actually, I have the happy faculty of being able to sleep with my eyes open and, in fact, I haven't heard any of your three speeches!"

Representative George Huddleston, Jr., of Alabama

⟪ I was making a political speech for a Congressman during a campaign, having flown to his district from Washington. The Congressman in Washington said nothing about the nature of the audience, nor did he when I arrived. However, just before I was introduced to the large audience, he leaned over and said, "Now this is a difficult assignment. We have here tonight the president of the

Women's Christian Temperance Union and some representatives of the Brewers' Association; the Chamber of Commerce and the CIO: the local president of the NAACP and
the Grand Dragon of the Ku Klux Klan. And," he said,
"you make them all vote for me."

About all left for me to talk on then was the Flag and
the Bible!

Representative William Jennings Bryan Dorn
of South Carolina

⟨[A deaf old couple were sitting on the porch one evening.
The old man attempted to tell his wife how much he appre-
ciated all she had done for him during their life. In her
deafness, she could not understand what he was trying to
tell her. At last, he shouted, "I'm proud of you!" She replied, "I'm tired of you, too!"

Senator John Sherman Cooper of Kentucky

⟨[In 1950, after two terms in the House, I ran for the
Senate but was defeated. I tried it again in 1954 with the
same result. When I announced my candidacy in 1956,
many people in my state—including some formerly close
supporters—said that I should not run in the primary because it was clear to everyone but me that I had no chance
at all of winning election.

It all reminded me of a story I had heard years earlier in
Colorado, a story that goes like this:

In the rugged high country of Colorado lived a shrewd
horse trader. One day a rancher with whom he had had
some dealings came by and complained:

"That horse you sold me last week is no good."

"Why do you say that?" asked the horse trader cautiously.

"He must not see very well," said the rancher. "The other day he trotted straight into the trunk of an aspen tree. Yesterday he walked into the creek as calm as you please, right up to his withers. And today he ran head first into a big rock outcrop over by the mesa. Why, I think that horse is stone blind."

"You're wrong," said the horse trader. "That horse ain't blind. He just don't give a darn."

Senator John A. Carroll of Colorado

❨ A parson in the cow country arrived at his prairie church on Sunday morning with a very thoroughly prepared sermon only to find one lonely parishioner, a cowboy, in his audience.

Being somewhat at a loss, he inquired of the cowboy as to whether he should proceed or simply pronounce the benediction. The cowboy replied, "If I went out to the pasture to feed my cattle and found only one cow, I believe I would feed her."

As a result, the minister delivered his prepared sermon and after the benediction stood at the door to shake hands with the congregation.

"How was it?" he asked the cowboy.

"Well," said the cowboy, "I believe if I took a load of hay down to feed my cattle and found only one cow, I don't believe I would give her the whole load."

Representative James E. Bromwell of Iowa

❨ Unswerving loyalty is acknowledged as the prime virtue in political relationships. A good example of such blind devotion is found in the story of an early-day Western politician, who was mulling the possibility of seeking reelection as Congressman.

He called in a slavishly devoted follower and suggested that the man poll some key citizens to determine his current political strength. The starry-eyed friend immediately set out on his assignment, pencil and pad in hand.

"Say," he said to the first citizen he met on the street, "old John Smith is thinking of running for Congress again. What do you think of him?"

Without hesitation, the citizen responded vehemently that he thought old John Smith was "an unscrupulous scoundrel devoid of intellect, decency and integrity, and an infamous plunderer whose sole aim in life is to feather his nest at the expense of the taxpayer."

"Thanks a lot," said the loyal pollster, as he wrote on his pad.

"I'll put you down on the doubtful list."

Senator Alan Bible of Nevada

❮ The new revenue agent had been assigned Patty's income tax return to audit. Not very much income and tax had been reported. So, when he saw under the charitable contributions section—"$1,000 to St. Mary's Church"—he naturally became curious. He asked the group chief what to do. "There's only one way to handle this," said the chief. "And that is to go out to see the pastor."

That afternoon, the chief passed by the agent's desk and saw him working on Patty's audit report. "Did you go see the pastor?" he asked. "Yes," said the agent. "I had a most interesting conversation with the pastor, too."

"Well," said the chief, "are you allowing the deduction?"

"Yes," said the agent, "I don't really think Patty contributed $1,000 to St. Mary's Church, but after my conversation with the pastor, I think that Patty will."

Senator Jack Miller of Iowa

❪ It seems that Zeke was in the habit of stopping at the corner bar too long, staggering home at all hours of the night. His wife, being of the husky variety, would generally administer a beating to Zeke on his arrival home. This did not seem to make an impression on Zeke because he would repeat the performance consistently. Finally, a neighbor lady said, "Mirandy, why don't you be nice to Zeke when he comes home. Maybe he will mend his ways." So the next time that Zeke staggered through the door, Mirandy met him, eased him over to the davenport, took off his shoes, and loosened his collar. She said, "Zeke, shall I kiss you, honey?" Zeke replied, "You might just as well, I'll catch heck when I get home anyway!"

Representative Ancher Nelsen of Minnesota

❪ An impecunious client approached the lawyer requesting the benefit of his legal services. The lawyer, apprehensive of the client's ability to pay a fee, raised this question in advance. The client stated that he had no money but could give the lawyer a barrel of oysters and three fine old Maryland hams. The lawyer felt that this was a reasonable retainer and agreed to take the case. Upon asking the nature of the charge against his new client, he was informed that it was grand larceny—the theft, of course, of a barrel of oysters and three fine old Maryland hams.

Representative Charles Mathias, Jr., of Maryland

❪ The candidate for Congress was addressing an assembly of inmates in an insane asylum when a voice from the rear of the hall shouted, "Lousy!"

The speaker paused, cleared his throat, and continued. Again, the same voice was heard louder than before, "LOUSY!"

The candidate glared, took a drink of water and then

went on with his remarks. And still again the rude retort rang out, "Lousy!"

The speaker turned to the superintendent and asked, "Shall I continue?"

"By all means," replied the superintendent, "this fellow has been here for over ten years, and this is the first time he has shown any signs of sanity."

                              Representative Stanley R. Tupper of Maine

(I went into a country store that was operated by a Democrat in one of the Republican counties west of the Blue Ridge Mountains. To the storekeeper I announced, "I'm Bill Tuck, Democratic nominee for Congress from the Fifth Virginia District. How are things up here for me?"

The storekeeper replied, "There just ain't no interest up here."

I continued to press him, hoping to get some favorable expression, and each time he made a similar reply. Finally, after I had pressed him to the point of exasperation, he said firmly, "There ain't no interest up here, and ain't none of them comin' out to vote, and the more of them that stay at home the better off you'll be!"

                              Representative William M. Tuck of Virginia

(During the latter part of my four-year term as Governor of Virginia, I was making an inspection tour of Virginia seafood resources. With me in the state yacht were the Virginia Commissioner of Fisheries and my executive assistant.

We stopped one night at a wharf on the Great Wicomico River in a community where I had been principal of a small country school prior to my enlistment in the U.S. Marines during World War I.

After dinner on the yacht, we strolled up to a nearby store, the only building in sight. A pleasant, housewifely type woman was behind the counter and I soon engaged her in conversation.

"I used to be principal of the school here," I informed her, recalling some of the more prominent of the pupils I had taught.

"What is your name?" she asked.

"Bill Tuck," I said, expecting her to recognize me as Governor.

"And what are you doing now, Mr. Tuck?"

Considerably deflated, I could give her but one answer. "I'm working for the state," I replied.

Representative William M. Tuck of Virginia

Oft, in the stilly night,
  Ere slumber's chain has bound me,
I think of things I should have said
  When others were around me.
And of such woeful waste of wit
  Constructively I weep,
And often in the still of night
  I kick myself to sleep.

Representative John Jarman of Oklahoma

(The first public office I held was County Superintendent of Education, to which I was elected at the age of twenty-five. Being young and inexperienced, I was under the impression that a speaker should speak at some length to make an impression on people that he was a man of knowledge. I was invited to make a commencement address in another county; and after speaking about forty-five minutes in a long, narrow school building where the acoustics were bad, I saw that in the back of the building people were going to sleep. Thinking that I would arouse them, I raised my voice and shouted, "Ladies and gentlemen, I want you to know that I am speaking for the future citizens of South Carolina." A man in the rear of the auditorium who had gone to sleep was aroused by my loud shout, and he shook his head and rose up and said, "Well, brother, if you speak much longer, they will soon be here, too."

Senator Strom Thurmond of South Carolina

◖ This is the story of how the Queen of Greece came to be called "honey child." That's the influence Alabama has. As a member of the Senate Foreign Relations Committee, I visit many countries. In Greece, I introduced myself to the Queen as Senator John Sparkman. "You should have said Senator John Sparkman of Alabama," another senator said after they had passed the Queen.

The Queen turned and said, "Oh! Are you from Alabama?"

I acknowledged that I was an Alabaman.

"Why, I met a young lieutenant recently," the Queen said, "and he said, 'I'm from Alabama, honey.' "

I replied, "He should have added the rest—honey child."

So the Queen of Greece was called "honey child" the rest of the night by everyone at the informal gathering.

Senator John J. Sparkman of Alabama

◖ I think the story that I have used the most over the years and that has always helped me to conclude a speech where there was going to be dancing and entertainment afterward is one concerning an introduction given me at a Rotary meeting by a nervous toastmaster.

It was an evening gathering and there was to be dancing and entertainment after I finished speaking. He nervously introduced me by saying, "Now we will hear from our *only* speaker and then we will have our *real* entertainment."

                    Senator Leverett Saltonstall of Massachusetts

❨ When I arose to address a Kiwanis Club in my district, the inevitable news photographer began to angle around for a good picture-taking position. The chairman of the meeting, worried for fear his main speaker might be distracted by popping flashbulbs, scurried over to the photographer and said impatiently, "Don't take his picture while he's speaking, shoot him before he starts."

                    Representative Howard W. Robison of New York

❨ During the course of one of my political campaigns in Alaska, one of my Fairbanks friends who was acting as master of ceremonies at a nonpartisan dinner we were attending told the following story about me:

A few days ago, Ralph attended the annual fair at Palmer, knowing, of course, that such a gathering was a most fertile field for shaking hands with a large number of potential voters in the forthcoming election. While feverishly making the rounds of the fairgrounds, Ralph came upon an old acquaintance he hadn't seen for quite a while, and said, "Well, hello, Joe; it's good to see you. Tell me, how's your father?" To which Joe replied, "I'm sorry to say, Ralph, he died last year." Ralph continued his handshaking tour of the fairgrounds and sometime later again came upon Joe. "Well, well, hello there, Joe; it's good to see you," said Ralph, "and how's your father?" To which Joe laconically replied, "Still dead!"

                    Representative Ralph J. Rivers of Alaska

❲ A quick-witted old gentleman who years ago represented his town in the Vermont Legislature was making an impassioned oration on the floor of the House of Representatives when suddenly his uppers flew out of his mouth. While the members laughed uproariously, he calmly proceeded to pick up his false teeth, wipe them off, replace them, and quietly wait for the laughter to subside.

With the attention of the House riveted on him, he received an ovation when he quietly said, "Gentlemen, that is the only thing false that has come out of my mouth today."

Senator Winston L. Prouty of Vermont

❲ As I grow older I find that I am one of the few men in most groups who wear a hat. I sometimes explain my hat by referring to the stranger who drove up in front of a hillside house in Arkansas and shouted to the boy on the gallery, "Son, where is your dad?" The boy replied, "Dad is down in the lot putting up the mules. You will know Dad; he is the one with the hat on."

Representative W. R. Poage of Texas

❲ I am a clergyman, and this is the reason for the appeal of the following story to me:

In a small Midwestern church one Sunday the regular minister was away. In his place a young man, just out of seminary, was asked to preach. Before starting his sermon he explained the term "substitute" by referring to the stained-glass windows. "If you will note the window, you will see some of the stained panes are missing. In their place some painted glass has been used. The painted glass is a substitute, and that is what I am today. Not a replacement, but a substitute."

After the service, as the young man stood at the door wishing all a good morning, a well-meaning parishioner paid him this dubious compliment: "You're no painted glass, you're a real pane."

Representative Henry C. Schadeberg of Wisconsin

⟨ One of my favorite stories, which did crop up in the course of legislative experience, concerns a time when I was serving in the Massachusetts Senate, and, although many might think it apocryphal, the incident actually did occur.

I received a note from an elderly lady living in a remote Berkshire County hill town who requested information regarding old-age assistance. Shortly thereafter, I had occasion to be near the town and thought I might drop by to see her.

She lived in a lonely farm house a good bit out of town and appeared to be a bright old soul quite able to handle herself. However, she was all alone, her husband having died a few years back and her children long since gone out on their own.

We sat down in the living room on a crisp day in January and she poured me a cup of steaming hot chocolate while I asked questions regarding her future plans. She told me that my information on old-age assistance had been most helpful, and said that she felt pretty well fixed up.

Shortly before leaving, I said, half-humorously, about the only thing I thought she needed was to get remarried in order not to be so lonely.

She looked at me and chuckled brightly, her eyes twinkling, and said she didn't really think so.

"After all," she said, pointing to the fireplace, "I have a roaring fire to keep me warm and there's the parrot to yell at me all day and my cat stays out all night. What else can a husband offer?"

Representative Silvio O. Conte of Massachusetts

❲ A Massachusetts colleague of mine once invited a distinguished Southern Congressman to speak at a fund-raising dinner in Boston. As there are many people who are prejudiced toward Catholics in the South, when his distinguished friend arrived, he explained "that Boston was chuck full of Irish Catholics, Polish Catholics, Italian Catholics, and French Catholics, and most of these were Democrats, and if he said anything against these people, they would lose Democratic support."

The Southern Congressman said, "Leave it up to me, I will take care of it."

Going into the hall and overwhelmed by the large crowd, he started his address stating "that he wanted them to know all the love, affection, and warmth in his heart for all those Irish Catholics, Polish Catholics, Italian Catholics, and French Catholics; the ones I have no use for are those darn Roman Catholics!"

Representative Silvio O. Conte of Massachusetts

❲ I had occasion to act as toastmaster for a convention of restaurant owners in Berkshire County, Massachusetts, last weekend as the result of an urgent request from the group's president.

One of my remarks included the frustration a Congressman meets in trying to please constituents with his behavior in Washington.

I noted that when I returned to the district to hold office hours, there were loud complaints that I was spending too much time there and should be working down in Washington. "That's what he was elected for," they said.

Then when I didn't make it back for several weeks, others said, "Who's that guy think he is? We only see him during elections."

When I came home shortly after being sworn in, driving

my old car, they were upset because it looked like something the farmers use to haul trash.

But, by gosh, when I bought a new one, they were sure the lobbyists had gotten to me already.

The first time I came home wearing an old suit from State Senate days, people said, "Look at him! Just an old bum!"

Yet when I bought a new suit, the first comment I heard was: "For crying out loud, he's gone 'high hat' with that Ivy League suit of his."

One Sunday I missed church because I was tied up talking with constituents and some people said that being down in Washington had made an atheist of me.

Several weeks later, when I was again back home and did get to church, they said, "Why that pious fraud! He's just trying to dig up votes."

To top it off, when I returned to my office Sunday night, waiting for me was a letter from a constituent. What did he have to say? That's right, he was complaining because I was spending too much time up in the district making personal appearances and holding office hours.

Representative Silvio O. Conte of Massachusetts

❐ The hotel clerk was losing his patience. "Look," he said, "I've told you a dozen times, we don't have any rooms. We're full."

"If President Johnson came," the man persisted, "you'd have room for him, wouldn't you?"

"Why, of course," the clerk admitted.

"Then let me have his room. He's not coming."

Representative Basil L. Whitener of North Carolina

⟨ I overheard two of my colleagues commenting on the President's State of the Union Message. One said the message had a lot of vision and sight. The other chap answered that he was being redundant—that there was no difference between vision and sight. The first fellow retorted that there certainly was a vast difference. "For example," he told the other, "last night we were out with two girls—mine was a vision and yours was a sight."

Representative Seymour Halpern of New York

⟨ I was invited to a large meeting in Jamaica, New York, largely inhabited by our Negro brethren. When I got to the meeting I found I was in Father Divine's Heaven. Not having been in heaven before, I honestly didn't know what to say. While I was sitting there collecting my thoughts, I found myself being introduced by an Angel (incidentally, that was the only time I have ever been introduced by an angel), who got up and shouted out "Seymour Halpern is our friend. He is a friend of the colored people. He knows our problems. His skin may be white but his heart is black."

Representative Seymour Halpern of New York

⟨ After I had delivered a speech at a political rally, one of the women in the audience approached me and, in glowing terms, remarked that she so enjoyed my talk and would very much like to have a copy. I told her that I was sorry that I had not prepared a text. Whereupon she asked, "Do you think that speech will ever be published?" I replied, "Perhaps posthumously," and she rejoined, "Oh, I hope that will be soon."

Representative Emanuel Celler of New York

❲ When I first ran for Congress, forty-three years ago, I sought to unseat a member who had been reelected several times. He resented my entering the field. He said at an outdoor meeting that I was just a kid and would not know my way around Washington and that I was not politically weaned. Then he added, "And, I'll tell you confidentially, he drinks and has a way with women." At that last crack, someone in the audience yelled, "Wonderful! We won't have to break him in."

Representative Emanuel Celler of New York

❲ The results of an election for sheriff in a small frontier town of the West were as follows: Cy Gummo, 300 votes; Clem Cadiddlehopper, 3 votes. Notwithstanding the obvious victory of his opponent, Clem showed up the next day in the general store, wearing two big six-guns and carrying a rifle. Immediately, one of the town loafers shot this remark at Clem: "Hey, Clem, you can't wear all those guns! You wasn't elected sheriff!" To which he got this reply: "I know I ain't sheriff, but if you had no more friends in this town than I do, you'd be wearing 'em too."

Representative Robert J. Corbett of Pennsylvania

❲ After one of the TVA lakes inundated the village of Butler, where I was born, a group of citizens was standing around in the courthouse yard in the county seat, and an elderly friend of mine was telling the group with considerable emotion that Butler, where Carroll Reece was born, was now 165 feet under water. One man in the crowd, who was not quite so emotional about me, asked, "How deep under water did you say Butler is where Carroll Reece was born?" He answered, "165 feet." The man replied, "Shucks, fire, that's not half deep enough!"

Representative Carroll Reece of Tennessee

⟨["Take good care of the property—just treat this house as though it were your own," I told my mother-in-law when I left on an overseas trip. "Did she?" was the question asked on my return. "Yes, she surely did," I replied. "She sold it!"

Representative Frank Chelf of Kentucky

⟨[When I am asked if I consider myself a true "feminist," I counter by telling the following story:

Seems that back in the days when women were struggling to win the right to vote, a rather strong-minded, thick-skinned old gal made it her mission to travel around her part of the country, giving speeches in support of the women's suffrage movement. Since these speeches invariably stirred up quite a controversy, she frequently spent the night in jail for inciting a riot.

After delivering a particularly fiery speech in a small town, the old gal found herself sharing a jail cell with a sweet young girl who was crying her eyes out. At first, the battle-hardened suffragette ignored the youngster's weeping, but finally the old gal's nerves began to wear thin. Patting the sobbing girl on the shoulder, the suffragette said, "There, there, Dearie, buck up! Things can't be as bad as all that. When you are in a situation like this, there's only one thing to do. Pray to God. SHE will help you."

Representative Catherine May of Washington

⟨[The other day I had some business with a colleague in the recently opened Rayburn Office Building. This is a magnificent structure, but because of its size there are some problems about getting around in the building. My secretary wrote out the following instructions for me: "Mr. de la Garza, to get to B-369, go down to the basement of this building and through the Longworth Building and down the escalators to the Rayburn Building. After going down the escalators to the Rayburn Building, go through the door and then go to the right and then to the left—go all the way down the hall and then to the left again and then turn right at the first hall on your right and all the way down that hall are the elevators on the right; go up the elevators to the basement floor. As you get off the elevator, turn right, then turn right again and go about fifty feet and then turn left, and there you are," she wrote. And sure enough, when I had made all these turns and twists, feeling as if I were a working crossword puzzle, there I was!

Representative Eligio de la Garza of Texas

❴ Two men caught the train together at Boise. Both men had purchased tickets to Pocatello.

For the first hundred miles or so, they both sat in deep silence, apparently reflecting upon their past, with some sense of guilt about past actions that they would like to forget. Finally, one of them turned to the other, introduced himself and said, "I may as well confess. I am just leaving the State Penitentiary at Boise. I was convicted some ten years ago for armed robbery. I have served my sentence and I am on my way home. I know it is a terrible thing to be an ex-convict and that is the reason I haven't said something to you before."

The other man thereupon replied, "You have nothing to be ashamed of. You have paid your debt to society; you can go home and walk with your head up. But as for me, I just completed a term as a Republican member of the State Legislature, and I can assure you I would a hell of a lot sooner face my friends and neighbors with a record like yours than mine."

Representative Ralph R. Harding of Idaho

⟨ During my first campaign for election as a member of the House of Representatives, back in 1956, we had open house at the Democratic Headquarters in Hutchinson, Kansas. Some 1,500 people gathered there to discuss politics and to drink coffee. The local newspaper printed a small article in the middle of the paper that stated: "Open house for breeding." Of course, I saw the article when it came out. About four in the afternoon, Mr. Jack Harris, the publisher of the paper, called me and said, "Congressman Breeding, how are you getting along with the party?" I said, "Just fine." He said, "Well, we have had more phone calls on the story than anything we have printed in recent months, mostly from old bachelors."

Representative J. Floyd Breeding of Kansas

⟨ "Well," snarled the tough old sergeant to the private, "I suppose after you get discharged from the Army you'll just be waiting for me to die so you can come and spit on my grave."

"Not me, Sarge," said the GI. "Once I get out of this Army, I ain't never standing in line again!"

Representative Harlan Hagen of California

⟨ There are many nationality groups located in my district. When they hold their annual picnics, the candidates are introduced and given the opportunity to give a speech.

During my first campaign, an eight-year-old came up to me after I had been introduced and made a brief statement.

Holding out his hand, he said, "Bill, that was a good speech —short."

I have made my remarks "short" ever since then.

Representative William H. Ayres of Ohio

(A certain public official had employed the same secretary for several years. After a particularly grueling campaign during which he received many comments on his good fortune in having such an efficient and willing secretary, the official decided to show his gratitude by giving the secretary a raise.

When the secretary noticed the increased amount of her check, she mentioned it to the boss. He replied that it was a reward for being such a faithful and valuable employee for so many years.

The secretary thoughtfully answered, "Then you have been short-changing me up until now, eh?"

[Former] Representative Hjalmar C. Nygaard of North Dakota

(Every fall I make a tour of my district, visiting each post office in my district and at each stop listening to the problems of all those who come. One afternoon, I had a long line of visitors on the front porch steps of the Lake Geneva Post Office (which also serves as a grocery store). The first little lady who came up didn't reply when I asked what her problem was, so I assumed she was deaf as she sat down beside me on the step and others vigorously pressed in for prompt attention. Finally, the last of them had left and I turned to the little lady and said in a loud voice, "Now what is your problem? The others have gone, and we can talk privately." The little lady looked up from where she had been sitting next to me all afternoon and said softly,

"Well, now, I am not deaf and I don't have any problems at all—but I sure did have a lot of fun this afternoon listening to all that stuff!"

Representative Charles E. Bennett of Florida

(A powerful Southern Democrat, who was a leader of conservatives in the House of Representatives, was once engaged in a heated debate with a Northern liberal.

During one exchange on the House floor, the Northern Democrat declared, "I hear the gentleman from the South finally has some primary opposition. I just want to tell him now that if he doesn't get my bill out of his committee, I shall go down to his district and campaign FOR him!"

Representative Albert Rains of Alabama

(The night of my general election victory in 1964, I determined that I should arrive at six in the morning the day succeeding the election to go to the steel mills at Sparrows Point, Gate No. 4, and welcome the workers into Bethlehem Steel and thank them for their support. I had been at the gates many times before, requesting the aid of the workers, and thought that my gesture would be well received.

I arrived at the gate at quarter to six and the response was warm—until one particular worker looked at me, backed off, and the following dialogue took place:

"You're Tydings, aren't cha?"

"Why, yes. I just wanted to thank you for your——"

"Don't thank me, buddy. I didn't vote for ya. Furthermore, I'm not gonna vote for ya, and finally, what're you doin' down here on taxpayers' time anyway, when you oughta be in Washington workin'?"

This was my first term, and I was not due to be sworn in until January, 1965.

Senator Joseph D. Tydings of Maryland

◖ A young soldier who unexpectedly had gotten a forty-eight-hour leave sought to improve his leave time by getting married. So, on a Saturday afternoon, he traveled to the county courthouse with his intended in tow. There, he found the county judge going over some papers in his chambers and explained to his honor that he wanted to get married. The judge, politely but firmly, told the young couple that while he would be delighted to perform the ceremony, this could not be done without a marriage license and that the marriage license office would not be open again until Monday.

"But, Your Honor," said the soldier, "couldn't you just say a few words to kind of tide us over the weekend?"

Representative Richard H. Poff of Virginia

◖ Nearly every family has legends it cherishes. I first heard this one when I went to a family reunion in Virginia.

An elderly member of the family still resided in the ancestral home. As he grew older and could farm less, he became more and more a devotee of following the hounds. He hunted and kept the hounds always beside him.

Not long ago he came home from a hunt in the evening, sat down beside a fireplace in his second-floor bedroom with favorite hounds around, and dozed off. When he awoke, the room was on fire. His first thought was his dogs. He started throwing them out the window. They would land on the slanting roof of a side room and slide to the ground. This worked very well except that this turned out to be more fun than the dogs had had in a long time. They started running back in the front door to get another chance at the slide.

The house was darned-near gone, says the legend, before the hunter realized he didn't have that many hounds.

Representative Earle Cabell of Texas

⟨ An old prospector happened across a group of Eastern dudes eating out and was asked to stop for some coffee. They kept pumping him for some of his experiences, and he decided to put it on for them. He told them of one adventure:

"There I was, trapped in a narrow canyon with a grizzly bear two yards away behind a tree, eyeing me. The only way to hit him was to ricochet a bullet off the high canyon wall on my right.

"So I gauged the windage, calculated the lead of the barrel and rate of twist, the hardness of the bullet and the angle of yaw it would have after smacking out of shape against the canyon wall. I judged the chances of nailing the bear about 90–20. A one-rail bank shot—a controlled ricochet. So I took aim and fired."

As the prospector paused, one excited tenderfoot asked, "Did you hit him?"

"Nope," the old man answered. "I missed the wall."

Representative Rodney M. Love of Ohio

⟨ During my first term in the House of Representatives, one afternoon I approached an elevator near which a young lad of about twelve was standing. As I pushed the "up" button, he announced that he had already pushed it. I expressed my thanks whereupon a prolonged silence ensued as we waited for the arrival of the elevator. I could feel the lad staring at me, when he broke the silence by abruptly inquiring, "Are you a Congressman?" I said yes.

"You know," he forlornly declared, "I can't tell a Congressman from a regular man."

> Representative Lucien N. Nedzi of Michigan

❨ One of my favorite stories concerns my colleague Representative John Culver of Cedar Rapids, who is now serving his first term in the House of Representatives.

As he was preparing to leave for Washington following his election last year, his children were staying at the home of their grandparents. The night before the journey east began, Representative Culver and his wife happened to peek through the door as their three youngsters were saying their bedtime prayers. The youngest one was saying, "Now I lay me down to sleep, I pray the Lord my soul to keep . . . God bless mommy, daddy, grandma and sister, and"— then added—"And now good-bye, God, we're going to Washington."

> Representative Stanley L. Greigg of Iowa

❨ Back in 1940, when Willkie ran against Roosevelt, the bootblack in my office building came into the office one morning to shine my shoes. He was wearing a large Willkie button on his lapel, and because of his apparent enthusiasm for Willkie, I tipped him generously. Two days later, I ran into the same bootblack in the elevator of the office building, and much to my surprise and shock, he was now wearing a Roosevelt button. I turned to him and said, "The other day you came into my office with a Willkie button, now you are wearing a Roosevelt button. Sam, what the heck are you? A Democrat or a Republican?" He looked at me with a smile, slapping his head and said, "I guess I'm a hypocrite."

> Representative Paul A. Fino of New York

❬ A farm boy became tired of not farming yet collecting his subsidy checks, and he thought he would like to work on the railroad. He went into the nearest town and applied for a job. The only position open was for a flagman, which the railroad desperately needed at that time. However, the employing agent thought he should give the young man a test to see how alert he was, so he submitted this question: "You are on the flagman's station, sitting in a chair and perhaps asleep when you hear a train whistle which awakens you. You look down the track and see Number One barreling down at 60 miles per hour. You turn and look up the track and the other way you see Number Two bearing down at 60 miles per hour. What would you do?"

Immediately, the boy replied, "I'd go get my brother."

"Why would you get your brother?" asked the employing agent.

The boy answered, "My brother ain't never seen a train wreck."

Representative J. Arthur Younger of California

❬ Following completion of the motion picture *Tomahawk*, a number of Sioux Indians who had taken part in the production toured the East and with their full war dress regalia advertised the premier showing of the film.

Ben American Horse, a Carlisle Institute graduate who at the time was in his late seventies or early eighties, was in charge of the Indian group. When they came to Washington, we wanted to do something nice for this old chief, who had down through the years been a very prominent Republican worker.

The South Dakota delegation took him to Vice-President Barkley's office, where Barkley showed him every respect due to a prominent First American. After sitting in Barkley's chair and visiting, he arose, took the Vice-President by the hand, and although Barkley was seventy-one years old at the time, Ben American Horse said, "Young man, let me give you a little advice. Be careful with your immigration laws. We were careless with ours."

Representative E. Y. Berry of South Dakota

《 Dr. Woo Ting Fan, accredited to the Government of the United States in 1900, was very fond of early morning walks.

Shortly after his arrival, Dr. Woo took his customary morning stroll along the streets of Washington, garbed in a beautiful embroidered silk robe with an equally gorgeous silk jacket and matching shoes. A short distance behind him were two American women debating whether he was a Chinese man or a Chinese woman. Unable to agree, they asked him, "Pray, tell us what are you? Are you a man or are you a woman?"

The minister charmingly smiled and replied, "Both of you are right. I am a lady's man."

Senator Hiram L. Fong of Hawaii

《 The year 1948 marked the hundredth anniversary of the first Angora goats ever to set foot on North American soil. A few were brought in from Turkey as a result of a special arrangement with the sultan.

I thought it would be appropriate to have a commemorative stamp struck off to do honor to the anniversary. Accordingly, I introduced a bill directing the Postmaster General to do that, and the bill was referred to the House Committee on Post Offices and Civil Service, of which Tom Murray of Tennessee was Chairman.

A month or two after the bill was introduced, I saw Tom in the hall and told him I had a little stamp bill in the committee that I would like for him to get some action on. Before I could tell him what it was, he told me that because of the large number of such bills being introduced, the Postmaster General had requested him to defer action on any individual stamp bills. Tom then added, "I would like to help you, and could probably do so if there were not so many frivolous bills of this kind introduced by members of the House. You know," he added, "some crazy gump introduced a bill to commemorate a goat!"

Representative O. C. Fisher of Texas